New Crafts

SHELLS

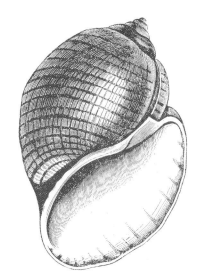

NEW CRAFTS
SHELLS
MARY MAGUIRE

PHOTOGRAPHY BY PETER WILLIAMS

LORENZ BOOKS
NEW YORK • LONDON • SYDNEY • BATH

For Bryony, and also Marie and Jill, who ensured her safe arrival in this world

THIS EDITION PUBLISHED IN 1997 BY LORENZ BOOKS, 27 WEST 20TH STREET, NEW YORK, NEW YORK 10011

LORENZ BOOKS ARE AVAILABLE FOR BULK PURCHASE FOR SALES PROMOTION AND FOR PREMIUM USE. FOR DETAILS, WRITE OR CALL THE MANAGER OF SPECIAL SALES: LORENZ BOOKS, 27 WEST 20TH STREET, NEW YORK, NEW YORK 10011; (212) 807-6739

ISBN 1 85967 376 7

PUBLISHER: JOANNA LORENZ
SENIOR EDITOR: JUDITH SIMONS
DESIGNER: LILIAN LINDBLOM
PHOTOGRAPHER: PETER WILLIAMS
STYLIST: GEORGINA RHODES
ILLUSTRATOR: VANA HAGGERTY

PRINTED AND BOUND IN HONG KONG

PICTURE ACKNOWLEDGEMENTS

The publishers would like to thank the following for additional images: page 8t, © The Horniman Museum, London; 8b, © The British Museum; 12, Private Collection/The Bridgeman Art Library, London; 9b, 9t, 10, John Bigelow Taylor, New York; 11t, © The Natural History Museum, London; 11b, reproduced by kind permission of the Marquess of Tavistock and the Trustees of the Bedford Estate; 13l, © The National Trust Photographic Library/Geoffrey Frosh; 13r, reproduced by courtesy of the Board of Trustees of the Victoria and Albert Museum.

10 9 8 7 6 5 4 3 2 1

CONTENTS

INTRODUCTION

SHELLCRAFT IS AT LAST BREAKING FREE FROM THE NEGATIVE ASSOCIATIONS OF SEASIDE SOUVENIRS AND IS BECOMING POPULAR WITH INNOVATIVE DESIGNERS AND CRAFTSPEOPLE. BEAUTIFUL OBJECTS IN THEIR OWN RIGHT, SHELLS ARE A VERSATILE ART MATERIAL THAT COMBINES WELL WITH OTHER NATURAL OBJECTS. SHELLS ARE THE PROTECTIVE HOMES OF SOFT-BODIED ANIMALS CALLED MOLLUSKS, WHICH SECRETE A LIQUID SUBSTANCE, CALLED *CONCHIOLIN*, THAT HARDENS WHEN EXPOSED TO AIR OR WATER. THERE ARE OVER 100,000 SPECIES OF MOLLUSK IN THE WORLD, EACH WITH ITS OWN DISTINCTIVE SHELL — RANGING FROM THE MINUSCULE TO THE ENORMOUS — IN AN AMAZING VARIETY OF SHAPES, COLORS AND TEXTURES. THE PROJECTS IN THIS BOOK EMPLOY A RANGE OF CRAFT TECHNIQUES, ENABLING YOU TO USE YOUR VACATION BEACHCOMBING FINDS TO MAKE BEAUTIFUL, PRACTICAL AND DECORATIVE ITEMS FOR THE HOME.

Left: The sheer variety of colors, shapes and textures found among shells makes them a fascinating and attractive medium for crafts.

HISTORY OF SHELLCRAFT

SINCE THE EARLY STONE AGE, HUMANS HAVE ADMIRED AND COLLECTED SHELLS AND USED THEM FOR VESSELS, TOOLS, WEAPONS, MUSICAL INSTRUMENTS, PERSONAL ADORNMENT, AND EVEN AS CURRENCY. SHELLS HAVE BEEN FOUND IN ARCHAEOLOGICAL SITES ALL AROUND THE WORLD, OFTEN VERY FAR FROM COASTAL AREAS. MOREOVER, THEIR INFLUENCE ON THE HUMAN WORLD HAS EXTENDED BEYOND THE REALM OF THE PHYSICAL: MOST SHELLS HAVE SOME KIND OF MYTH OR LEGEND ATTACHED TO THEM AND THEIR SUPPOSED POWERS, AND THEY HAVE BEEN USED FOR FORTUNE-TELLING AND DIVINATION PURPOSES FOR CENTURIES.

One of the first musical instruments is thought to have been a conch shell; by making a hole in its side, the shell can be used as a trumpet. The best-known shell for this purpose is called a Triton's Trumpet. Wind chimes, maracas and other percussion instruments have also been made from shells.

Shells appear in the oldest jewelry, either shaped into beads or with the centers ground out so they could be worn as bracelets. Some shells simply had a single hole pierced in them to form necklaces, and they were sometimes covered with a pigment such as ocher.

Patterns have been etched into and shapes have been carved from shells in all manner of ways. They have also been used for mosaics and inlays, but their biggest decorative use has always been for personal adornment. They been incorporated into the costumes of many peoples, especially those of Oceania, which, with its myriad islands and plentiful supply of sumptuous shells, has wonderful examples of jewelry and costumes.

No shell has been more implicated in human history than the cowrie. In ancient

Above: This is a classic example of a conch shell trumpet - it dates from the eighteenth century and was made in India.

Left: All these items of decorative shellwork date from the first half of the second millennium BC and were found in Nubia, a once prosperous Egyptian colony on the trade route between the Mediterranean and tropical Africa. The girdle is made of shell-disc beads, and the finger ring is a mere ⅛ inch thick.

durable, shell and is therefore ideal for transportation and trading purposes. It has circulated in more parts of the world than any modern currency with perhaps the exception of our own dollar.

The uibangwa shell was believed to act as a powerful charm. Rarely used whole, its circular ends were cut off to make discs, which were smoothed down, leaving the shell's natural internal spiral intact to act as a relief pattern. This shell was an important element in central African jewelry, indicating wealth and status, and was often worn on the forehead. In an attempt to break the connection with

Left: This stunning piece, made of silver and cowrie shells, is from Tamil Nadu, India, and is used to decorate the horns of a water buffalo in a secret native ceremony.

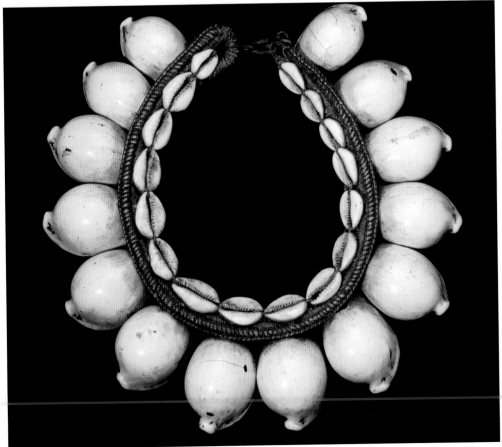

Egypt, it was regarded as a half-closed, ever-watchful eye and was therefore used as protection against the evil eye – a belief so powerful that it has survived to this day in parts of Africa and the Mediterranean. Cowrie shells have even been hung from the prows of ships as protectors and direction finders.

In Africa, cowrie shells were seen to represent a woman's reproductive organs and were used in fertility rites; in ancient Rome they were associated with the goddess Venus. At festivals in Rome they were carried around on poles accompanied by phallic symbols to bestow fertility on the onlookers. Cowries were also often stuck onto African and Oceanic carvings, giving them a wonderful textural quality and adding symbolic significance.

But the cowrie shell is best known for its usage as currency, especially the money cowrie found on the Maldive Islands. It is a small and lightweight, but extremely

Right: A man's necklace made of cowrie shells from the remote islands of Tanimbar, Indonesia.

paganism, colonial missionaries broke thousands of these uibangwa. Shells were also fashioned into discs in New Guinea, where they were worn suspended from the nose. In Mauritius, women wore them in their hair, and Tibetans wore them in their ears. The ancient Egyptians ground out the center and used them as bracelets.

The scallop shell played an important role in the history of arts and crafts, more for its inspirational effect as a motif and symbol than in itself. During the Middle Ages, the scallop shell became associated with St. James, and he is often depicted wearing it; it became known as the "pilgrim shell" because it was worn by pilgrims as proof that they had been to the Holy Land. During the Renaissance, it became a popular motif in ceramics, sculpture, painting and, most importantly, architecture.

During Roman times, royal purple dye was obtained by crushing muricid snail shells and extracting the dye-producing gland. It took such vast quantities of these snails to make a tiny amount of dye that it was said to be worth more than gold, and only the emperor and top officials were allowed to wear it. Most amazing of all was the production of yarn from the byssus threads that anchor some types of clam shells to the sea bed. It was woven into a fabric known as "cloth of gold," which is thought to be the Golden Fleece of Greek mythology.

Sophisticated craftworking techniques have also been applied to shells, such as etching, engraving, lapidary arts and the carving of cameos, with stunningly intricate results. In the eighteenth century, Sailors' Valentines were very popular. These were intricate mosaics of tiny shells

Left: Male and female ceremonial necklaces from the Philippines with butterfly-shaped mother-of-pearl pendants.

in octagonal boxes and were said to have been made by sailors for their sweethearts. In fact, they were manufactured by a small industry in Barbados.

A wonderful episode in the history of shellcraft was the creation of the grotto. The earliest grottoes were made in renaissance Italy and were dark, cave-like places in which to ponder philosophy and poetry. Made from oyster shells, pumice chips and volcanic ash, they were then coated with green wax to look like shiny moss – in, the floors of later grottoes were often covered with moss. During the seventeenth century, grottoes spread to France and Austria, eventually reaching England, where they became such a craze with the landed gentry that half the stately homes in Britain had one. They varied from large architectural pavilions covered with patterns in shell marquetry, to fantastic organic shapes encrusted with shells and spar, with cascades of mirrors and stalactites of crystal.

By the time of the Industrial Revolution, the middle classes had developed their own equivalent of the grotto, a remarkable example of which can be seen in Devon,

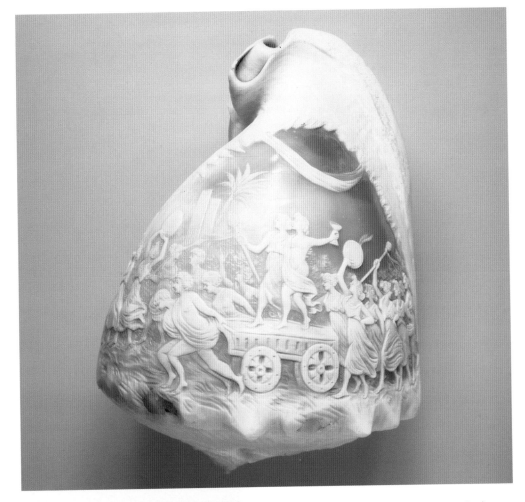

Above: The Helmet Shell, along with the Giant Conch, is ideally suited to the creation of cameos. This exquisite example was carved in Italy from a shell from Madagascar.

Left: The grotto at Woburn Abbey in Bedfordshire, England, which was constructed for the Fourth Earl of Bedford in the first half of the seventeenth century. The designer may have been Inigo Jones, the man who planned the first London square, Covent Garden Piazza, at about this time.

England. The Parminter sisters encrusted the walls of their house, "A la Ronde," with shells, feathers and seaweed, all gathered at the local seashore.

During Victorian times, shellcraft was recommended as a genteel pastime for ladies of leisure. Arrangements of shells were made and placed under glass domes, pictures were composed and stuck onto silk backgrounds or embedded in wet plaster around mirrors and frames and on trinket boxes.

As the seaside vacation became an established annual practice, a lucrative cottage industry in shellcraft developed at resorts, and all manner of knickknacks were made to sell to tourists to take home as souvenirs. Although the geography and economics of the industry have changed enormously over the years, the products have remained much the same. It is this aspect that is most often associated with shellcraft.

A NOTE ABOUT CONSERVATION
Shells are a wonderful resource for craftworkers, but one that is too often exploited. The excesses of the shellcraft industry have led to the scarcity, if not extinction, of some species. Most shells and corals for sale at stores were collected while the animal was still alive – which is why they look so shiny, colorful and per-fect. Collecting live shells does disrupt the balance of nature, so only gather shells when the animal has died, or abandoned its home, and do not collect any shells in conservation areas. When buying shells, choose only those you know to be waste products from the fishing industry, or that come from a sustainable and well-managed source.

Some countries are making efforts to regulate their shell trade and have intro-duced legislation protecting particular

species, such as giant clams, Triton's Trumpet, Imperial Harp, Horned Helmet, Queen Conch, Tiger Cowrie and Chambered Nautilus; others have imposed a complete ban on the collecting of live shells. For more information, contact your national Marine Conservation Society (see addresses at back of book).

Above: Victorian artists were both knowledgable and often eccentric users of shells. Here they are used with several other materials in a surreal collage.

Above: A decorative featherwork and shell panel from the Shell Gallery at "A la Ronde", created by the Parminter sisters for their own home.

Left: The Bonnell Vase, completed in 1781 by Mrs Beale Bonnell and Miss Harvey Bonnell. It stands two feet high, and it is composed of 300 bunches of flowers, all made out of shells painstakingly collected by Mrs Bonnell. It is thought to have been one of a pair, the other of which was given to Queen Adelaide.

GALLERY

SHELLCRAFT SEEMS TO HAVE EARNED A BAD NAME IN THE PAST AND HAS BEEN ASSOCIATED WITH "TACKY TRINKETS." SHELL-ENCRUSTED SEASIDE MEMENTOES DO HAVE THEIR OWN KITSCH AESTHETIC BUT ARE HARDLY INSPIRING TO THE CRAFTWORKER. HOWEVER, DESIGN STORES AND MAGAZINES NOW BEAR WITNESS TO THE POPULARITY OF SHELLS AND SHELL MOTIFS, AND CONTEMPORARY CRAFTSPEOPLE ARE BEGINNING TO APPRECIATE THEIR ARTISTIC POTENTIAL. THESE PHOTOGRAPHS DEMONSTRATE THE RANGE OF WORK BEING DONE WITH SHELLS, FROM THE RETROSPECTIVE, GROTTO-LIKE INTERIORS OF BELINDA EADE TO THE CONTEMPORARY UNION OF NATURAL AND MAN-MADE MATERIALS IN BRIDGET MORRALL'S WORK. THE AIM IS TO INSPIRE YOU IN YOUR OWN SHELL CREATIONS.

Right: CANDELABRA AND BRACELET
To make the candelabra, which measures 14 x 11 inches, Stefano first solders pieces of metal together to give the coral shape, then sprays on colored sand to finish. To make the bracelet, Stefano links together blown glass leaves, gilded metal, and real shells, in the style that characterizes all his work.
STEFANO POLETTI

Left: BIG MIRROR
This mirror, which measures 25 x 24½ inches, was simply made using a wooden frame base, hardboard and tile adhesive, into which Clare has embedded shells collected from beaches around the world and other found objects. She has then varnished it to bring out the natural colors of the shells and to protect the frame. Clare has always loved shells and started collecting them at an early age. She finds that their intricate beauty makes them exquisite natural works of art.
CLARE TOTTEM

Below: MARINE NECK COWL
Susie constructs her work by hand on an industrial knitting machine; she creates a transparent fabric with rows of small pockets trapping small objects. This piece incorporates shells and polished stones into a fine mesh, which is fashioned into a loop to be worn around the neck.
SUSIE FREEMAN

Right: MARY'S JEWELRY
This set of jewelry is made from shells recycled from old necklaces. The brooch and earrings are formed from small abalone shells with rock crystal pebbles inside. The necklace has multiple strands of small pearls laced into pearly snail shells, and smooth fragments of these have been used to complete the piece.
MARY MAGUIRE

Left: SHELLY PHONE
Andrew prefers to use shells as integral elements of his designs rather than merely as decoration. This working telephone, the dimensions of which are 16 x 8 inches, is constructed from a dismantled modern phone. The base is made from driftwood mounted on cockle-shell feet, and it has a beached starfish support for the hammered copper pipe stem. The earpiece is set into a murex shell, and the mouthpiece is enclosed in a scallop shell, which has perforations to allow for speaking. The keyboard is from the original phone, but the plastic has been removed to expose the rubber membrane, and fish vertebrae have been glued on to act as buttons.
ANDREW GILLMORE

Above: BEACHBALL LIGHT
The light measures 4¼ x 4¼ inches. Bridget takes her inspiration from the things she finds along the seashore, from beautiful shells to plastic bottles. She finds that the items she discovers often take on a more interesting aspect when put into unlikely contexts. She is fascinated by the tension between man-made objects and natural pieces, and she exploits this in her work.
BRIDGET MORRALL

Opposite: BELINDA'S GROTTO
This garden-room grotto incorporates tufa, knapped-flint and basalt as a framework, with panels of abalones, cockles and various "donated shells." The guardian nymphs are of oysters, cockles, mussels and red porphyry. The long mirrors give the illusion of worlds beyond.
BELINDA EADE

Above: PETER'S LAMP
The inspiration for this lamp, the height of which is approximately 15 inches, came from the memory of watching flamenco dancers while on vacation in Spain. Its framework is created by three twisted pieces of driftwood that have been doweled and screwed together to form a sort of pyramid. A bulb-holder was fitted into the center, and shells were attached in position on the wood to screen the bulb.
PETER WILLIAMS

Left: PINK BOX
Peter found the glitter in a box of assorted things bought at an auction; it was labeled "For shell making" and dated 1784. Peter took up the challenge and decorated this box, which is 8 x 5 inches. He originally used restored antique boxes, but now he has them specially made.
PETER COKE

Above: SHELL CUPBOARD
Marc makes a range of furniture in painted wood, such as the cupboard featured here, which measures 19 x 16 inches. He incorporates shells into his work to create a Mediterranean look. Most of his pieces are for bathrooms, as he feels they provide the perfect backdrop for the natural beauty of shells.
MARC SALAMON

Above: MIRROR
This mirror is mounted on a cut-out wooden base; the smaller shells have been glued on with a water-based glue and the larger ones with a glue gun.
PETER COKE

Below: SAILOR'S VALENTINE
Peter started working with shells about ten years ago when he began restoring early 19th-century sailors' Valentines; this one measures 12 x 12 inches. Since then he has been collecting minuscule shells from all over the world. His wonderful designs are inspired by the patterns on antique French carpets.
PETER COKE

MATERIALS

THE PROJECTS IN THIS BOOK HAVE BEEN DESIGNED WITH THE ENVIRONMENT IN MIND, SO THE TYPES OF SHELLS USED HAVE BEEN COLLECTED IN A RESPONSIBLE WAY FROM THREE MAIN SOURCES: THE FISHING INDUSTRY AND RESTAURANTS, BEACHCOMBING AND OLD SHELL NECKLACES. OTHER NATURAL OBJECTS FOUND ON THE BEACH MAKE ATTRACTIVE MATERIALS FOR SHELLCRAFT PROJECTS AND ARE ALSO IN KEEPING WITH A SEASIDE THEME.

Assorted shells Oyster, scallop, cockle and mussel shells are all regularly discarded from restaurants and can be easily recouped if you become friendly with your local seafood restaurant and ask them to save them for you. Periwinkles, limpets and many other types of shells can often be found washed up on the beach. Beachcombing is a pleasant vacation activity, but be sure to pick up only the empty shells, as others may still have a living creature within. If you are lucky enough to find a dried-out dead starfish, it will make a lovely addition to a shellcraft project, but don't be tempted to buy them, as they will have been fished for the purpose. Large land snail shells are also attractive and one is used in the Fountain project. In many parts of the world, snails are eaten and the shells discarded.

Cotton rope This type of rope is used in the Wreath and Tassels projects. It comes in a wide range of thicknesses and colors, and its natural appearance complements shells beautifully.

Driftwood You can find driftwood in beautiful sea-sculpted shapes. It is best to look along the high-tide mark on rocky beaches, where it tends to get trapped.

Feathers Try to find feathers in interesting colors. They look wonderful with shells in many decorative projects.

Paper Use handmade or recycled paper from craft or stationery shops, as it looks better with natural materials.

Polyboard Polyboard is perfect for making items such as the cover of the Vacation Album and the face of the Sandcastle Clock, as it is both lightweight and fairly thick. It can also be folded easily by scoring with a scalpel.

Raffia This natural material combines easily and effectively with shells, and it is widely available at craft stores and garden centers.

Ribbons Choose ribbons with a seaside feel, such as checks and stripes, for your shellcraft projects or to match the colors of the shells.

Sand Small amounts of sand are useful for some shellcraft projects. It can be bought from builder's merchants or at children's toy stores as "play sand."

Seaweed Often found along the high-tide mark, there are many different types of seaweed. It has a strong odor and therefore best used for outdoor projects.

Shell necklaces Old and broken shell necklaces are a useful source of smaller shells. They are cheap and easy to find at flea markets, antique stores and second-hand stores. Recycling shells in this way is both economical and environmentally friendly.

Stone-effect beads These natural-looking beads come in a variety of shapes and shades and combine well with shells.

String Use natural string bought at gardening and hardware stores for shell mobiles and candelabras.

Weathered pebbles Pebbles that have been worn by the sea are attractive in their own right. Try to find pebbles with holes worn right through them, as this makes them easy to attach to hanging projects, such as the Mobile and Chandelier.

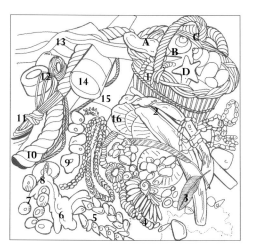

KEY
1 Basket of assorted shells
  A oyster shell
  B large land snail shell
  C large periwinkle shell
  D beached starfish
2 Driftwood
3 Feathers
4 Sand
5 Old shell necklaces
6 Seaweed
7 Limpet shells
8 Stone-effect beads
9 Weathered pebbles
10 Cotton rope
11 Raffia
12 String
13 Ribbons
14 Paper
15 Polyboard
16 Scallop shells

EQUIPMENT

Don't be put off by the array of equipment shown here — this is what you would need to make every project in the book. Only a very few items of equipment are essential for shellcraft, and you will probably find you have most of them in your household tool box already. Two additional items in which you may have to invest are a mini-drill and adhesive tile grout.

Adhesive tile grout This type of grout is excellent for mosaic and embedding work. The kind with adhesive will hold the shells most securely in place. Apply it with a palette knife.

Angle brackets Useful for holding together pieces of wood joined at an angle, these are used on the roof ridge of the Playhouse.

Bench hook A simple homemade bench hook is a useful device for sawing (see Basic Techniques).

Compass Use this for marking up the design for mosaic or other decorative patterns.

Corrugated fasteners These are a quick and easy way of joining planks together (see Scallop-hinged Cupboard project).

Craft knife Use a craft knife when more pressure is needed than a scalpel could provide.

Double-sided carpet tape This is stronger than most double-sided tapes and can be used to hold cardboard and fabrics together.

Drill Use this tool to make larger holes in less delicate shells such as scallops.

Dust mask Wear a mask when sanding shells to protect yourself from dust.

Epoxy putty This is an adhesive putty that comes in two parts to be mixed together just before use. It sticks very strongly and so is ideal for tough joining purposes. Once dry, it can be sanded and drilled.

Epoxy resin glue This is a strong glue useful for the construction of craft pieces.

Files An assortment of files is useful for filing off rough edges or making holes in shells bigger when drilling would be too heavy-handed.

Galvanized wire This type of wire is available at good hardware stores and is used for threading through the cotton rope to make the Wreath.

General-purpose pliers These are useful for shaping and manipulating sturdier types of wire.

Hammer This tool will come in handy for attaching shells to their bases and mounting finished pieces.

Hinges These are needed for projects that have doors, such as the Scallop-hinged Cupboard and the Playhouse.

Hole punch The type of hole punch used for leather can also be used for punching holes in paper and stiff fabrics.

Hot glue gun This is useful for gluing shells and other items onto curved surfaces, if the glue needs to set quickly.

Instant bonding adhesive The gel form of this glue is much easier to control than the ordinary type.

Jewelry pliers Use these for shaping fine wire.

Masking tape This is useful for a number of purposes, including holding pieces together while the glue dries.

Mini-drill This is the most useful tool to invest in for shellcraft. It will enable you to drill small and even tiny holes in the most fragile of shells. Attachments are also available for sanding off rough surfaces, grinding rough edges and polishing shells until they shimmer (see Basic Techniques).

Mini-drill attachments These include a wool attachment for polishing, grinders, a felt polishing attachment, a sanding disc and attachments, and drill bits.

Paintbrushes Keep a range of different sizes of paintbrushes for large and small painting jobs.

Protective gloves Gloves should be worn when using epoxy putty to avoid contact with the hands.

Protective goggles Wear these to protect your eyes when drilling, grinding or sanding shells.

Reusable adhesive Use this for holding small shells to the work surface to prevent them from slipping as you drill into them.

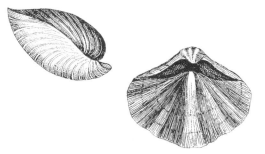

Saw Various saws are used for the wood construction in some of the projects, including an electric jigsaw, a tenon saw and a hacksaw.

Scalpel A scalpel is useful for cutting fine lines in cardboard, fabrics, etc.

Scissors General household scissors are sufficient for most shellcraft projects.

Screwdriver This tool will be helpful in projects that include hinges, for example.

Screws, nails and bolts It is a good idea to have a range of these in your tool box for use in those projects that are made from wood and fiberboard.

Tweezers Use tweezers for picking up tiny shells in mosaic work.

White glue This glue is perfect for attaching shells, and it dries transparent.

Wire-cutters These are essential for cutting wire to the required length.

Wood glue This can be used for the same purposes as white glue.

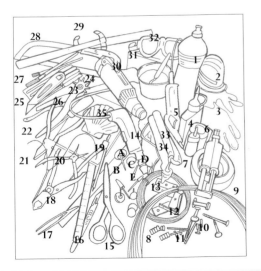

KEY
1 White glue
2 Dust mask
3 Protective gloves
4 Epoxy resin glue
5 Wood glue
6 Double-sided carpet tape
7 Instant bonding adhesive gel
8 Galvanized wire
9 Masking tape
10 Screws, nails and bolts
11 Corrugated fasteners
12 Angle brackets
13 Hinges
14 Mini-drill and attachments
  A wool mop
  B grinders
  C felt mops
  D sanding disc and attachment
  E drill bits
15 Scissors

16 Scalpel
17 Tweezers
18 Wire-cutters
19 Compass
20 Jewelry pliers
21 General-purpose pliers
22 Bench hook
23 Screwdriver
24 Hole punch
25 Craft knife
26 Files
27 Paintbrushes
28 Saw
29 Hammer
30 Drill
31 Adhesive tile grout and palette knife
32 Protective goggles
33 Epoxy putty
34 Reusable adhesive
35 Hot glue gun

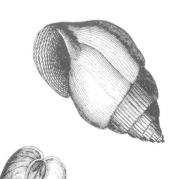

BASIC TECHNIQUES

SHELLS ARE NATURALLY BEAUTIFUL OBJECTS AND REQUIRE FEW TECHNIQUES TO EMBELLISH THEM, EXCEPT PERHAPS FOR SANDING OFF ROUGH SURFACES TO REVEAL THE MOTHER-OF-PEARL UNDERNEATH, POLISHING THEM TO MAKE THEM GLEAM, OR GRINDING DOWN ROUGH EDGES. WHAT SHELLS DO NEED IS A METHOD OF ATTACHING THEM TO THE BASE OF YOUR CHOSEN PROJECT. THE BEST WAY IS TO DRILL A HOLE THROUGH THE SHELL, THEN THREAD, SEW, WIRE OR NAIL THE SHELL IN PLACE. THIS SECTION DEMONSTRATES THE SKILLS YOU NEED TO DO THE SHELLCRAFT PROJECTS IN THIS BOOK AND TO TAKE THE CRAFT FURTHER.

VARNISHING

Shells coated with a thick varnish are an all too common sight. This is unnecessary and spoils the shells; if you want to emphasize their natural color, use a thin, clear oil, such as baby oil. Thin it down with lighter fluid and apply with a brush or cotton ball.

PAINTING

Inks containing shellac are ideal for painting shells. They can be mixed or watered down to achieve subtle hues and, once dry, the color is waterproof. You can also use watercolors, but you will need to varnish them if the shells are to be used outdoors.

DRILLING

Before you start drilling, make sure the shells are secured to your work surface with reusable tacky putty. Hold them firmly in place as you drill.

Drilling larger shells

Holes large enough for a nail to pass through can be made using an ordinary drill.

Drilling small shells

Drill bits ranging from small to tiny are available for mini-drills and can be used for drilling small shells. The more fragile the shell, the finer the drill bit should be and the slower the speed of the drill. Judging the right place to make a hole is often a matter of instinct. Generally, it is best to drill small conch shells through the bottom of the mouth of the shell from the inside. Drill small cockle shells through the tip also from the inside.

GRINDING

There are a wide range of grinding attachments available for mini-drills, and it is handy to have a couple, one pointed and one straight-edged. These can be used for smoothing jagged edges and removing remaining bits of cartilage. Always wear a dust mask and goggles when doing this type of work.

Pointed grinder

Use this attachment for grinding out the black deposit left inside scallop shells. You will need to do this for the Scallop Sconce project.

Straight-edged grinder

Run this attachment along the rough edges of shells to smooth them. Don't hold the drill still for too long as it will quickly eat a groove into the shell.

SANDING AND POLISHING

Amazing results can be achieved by
sanding and polishing the surfaces of ordinary shells such as these green mussels.
Always wear a dust mask and goggles
when doing this sort of work.

Sanding

1 Using a coarse-grade sanding disc,
  sand off the greeny-black shell coating
to reveal a brownish layer.

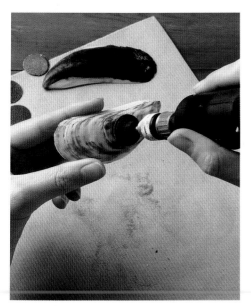

2 Continue to sand, smoothing down
  the ridges.

3 Switch to a fine-grade sanding disc to
  strip the shell down to the mother-of-
pearl. Be careful at this stage, as the shell
will now be very fragile.

Polishing

Various felt, wool and cotton mop heads
can be bought for mini-drills and will help
you put a shimmer on your shells. First
wash the shells and dry them thoroughly.

1 Use a wool mop head to shine the inner
  body of the shell.

2 To get into the corners, use a
  conically-shaped felt mop.

SAWING

1 When sawing flat scallops for the edges
  of the Playhouse roof, a bench hook is
very useful. One can be made using a square
of wood onto which you nail a baton at the
end of one side, positioning a scallop on the
other. Hammer in a nail on either side of it
to hold the shells in place while you are
sawing; the "hook" over the bench will prevent the wood from moving around. Use a
hacksaw and start by sawing gently along
the center line.

SHELL DRAWER KNOBS

THIS SIMPLE PROJECT TRANSFORMS A PLAIN SET OF WOODEN DRAWERS INTO AN EYE-CATCHING PIECE OF FURNITURE. THE DISTRESSED PAINTWORK FINISH IS EASIER TO ACHIEVE THAN IT LOOKS AND GIVES THE CHEST OF DRAWERS A SUBTLY AGED APPEARANCE THAT WORKS WELL IN COMBINATION WITH THE SHELLS. EXTEND THE SHELL THEME TO MAKE DOOR KNOBS FOR CUPBOARDS AND WARDROBES IN EXACTLY THE SAME WAY BUT USING LARGER SHELLS AND SCREWS.

1 Wearing protective gloves, combine the two parts of the epoxy putty and fill the backs of the shells with it. Embed the heads of the screws in the putty as deeply as possible. Let dry.

3 Run over the painted surface of the chest of drawers randomly with a wax candle to give the second coat of paint a mottled effect.

5 Rub the paintwork with steel wool to expose the undercoat in places. At the edges, rub down to the wood.

2 Paint the chest of drawers with the darker shade of green paint and let dry.

4 Paint the chest of drawers with the lighter shade of green paint and let dry.

6 Saw six ½-inch lengths of bamboo. Thread a piece of bamboo onto the screw embedded inside each shell. Drill a hole in the front of each drawer and screw on the knobs.

MATERIALS AND EQUIPMENT YOU WILL NEED

PROTECTIVE GLOVES • EPOXY PUTTY • SIX COCKLE SHELLS • SIX SCREWS • SMALL CHEST OF DRAWERS •
LATEX PAINT: TWO SHADES OF GREEN • PAINTBRUSH • WAX CANDLE • STEEL WOOL • SAW • BAMBOO CANE • DRILL

SEASHORE CARDS

RECEIVING A CARD THAT HAS BEEN MADE FOR YOU IS SO SPECIAL THAT IT MAKES THE CARD A GIFT IN ITSELF. USE THE CARD AS THE BASE IN WHICH TO FRAME PRETTY SHELLS FOUND ON A SEASIDE STROLL. TINY STARFISH ARE BEAUTIFUL BUT ARE RARELY FOUND BEACHED; FOR ECOLOGICAL REASONS, DO NOT BE TEMPTED TO BUY THEM. YOU CAN MAKE YOUR OWN LOOK-ALIKES FROM CUT-OUT SANDPAPER, WHICH EFFECTIVELY CONVEYS THE TEXTURE OF STARFISH. THE ENVELOPE COMPLETES THE GIFT, STITCHED TOGETHER WITH RAFFIA AND HELD CLOSED BY A FEATHER THREADED THROUGH A WEATHERED LIMPET SHELL.

1 Fold a sheet of paper in half to make a card. Tear two squares from paper in contrasting colors, one smaller than the other.

3 Glue the smaller square in the center with white glue. Glue on some seaweed and a shell.

5 Cut a rectangle of paper with a triangular flap at one end – the rectangle should be large enough when folded to hold the card. Fold the envelope and stitch the sides together. Start stitching at the bottom and continue to the point of the flap, leaving a loose end of raffia.

2 Thread a darning needle with raffia and sew the larger square onto the card with a running stitch around the edge.

4 Back a piece of fine sandpaper with double-sided sticky tape. Cut out starfish shapes, remove the backing paper from the tape and stick one starfish in each corner. Glue a small shell in the center of each starfish.

6 Tie a limpet shell onto the end of the two loose strands of raffia. Wrap the raffia around the envelope and thread the feather through the raffia under the limpet to hold the envelope closed.

MATERIALS AND EQUIPMENT YOU WILL NEED

ASSORTED HANDMADE PAPERS • DARNING NEEDLE • RAFFIA • SCISSORS • WHITE GLUE • SEAWEED • ASSORTED SHELLS •
FINE SANDPAPER • DOUBLE-SIDED STICKY TAPE • WEATHERED LIMPET SHELL WITH HOLE • FEATHER

SUNBLEACHED WREATH

WREATHS ARE TRADITIONALLY HUNG ON DOORS AS A SIGN OF WELCOME. THEIR CIRCULAR SHAPE SYMBOLIZES ETERNITY, SO IT IS APPROPRIATE TO USE THEM TO REFLECT THE SEASONS. WE ARE ALL FAMILIAR WITH THE HOLLY AND IVY WREATHS OF CHRISTMASTIME, BUT HOW NICE IT IS TO BE REMINDED OF THOSE RELAXING DAYS BY THE SEA ON A DULL DAY BACK AT HOME. HERE, WHITE COTTON ROPE FORMS THE BASE OF THE WREATH, BUT A LENGTH OF OLD, WORN ROPE WOULD BE EVEN BETTER, IF YOU MANAGE TO FIND ONE ON THE BEACH. CHOOSE A LENGTH OF RIBBON THAT FITS IN WITH THE SEASIDE THEME TO FINISH THE WREATH.

1 Bind both ends of the length of rope with masking tape to avoid unraveling. Using the wire-cutters, cut a piece of galvanized wire a little longer than the length of cotton rope. Insert the wire into one end of the rope.

2 Twist the rope around the wire and push the wire along until you reach the other end of the rope. The wire should now be forming a core along the center of the rope. Bend the rope into a circle.

3 Insert each protruding wire into the opposite end of rope, so that the wires poke through the rope. Bend a hook at the end of each wire, using pliers, and push the hooks into the core of the rope.

4 Wrap double-sided sticky tape around the seam and cover by winding white string around it. ▶

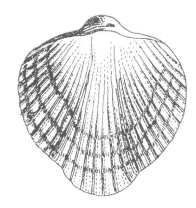

MATERIALS AND EQUIPMENT YOU WILL NEED

THICK COTTON ROPE, 27½ INCHES LONG • MASKING TAPE • WIRE-CUTTERS • GALVANIZED GARDEN WIRE • PLIERS •
DOUBLE-SIDED STICKY TAPE • WHITE STRING • ASSORTED SHELLS • REUSABLE TACKY PUTTY • MINI-DRILL • DARNING NEEDLE • RAFFIA •
GLUE GUN AND GLUE STICKS • WHITE GLUE • ASSORTED DRIED FLOWERS IN SUBTLE COLORS • WIDE RIBBON

5 Drill holes in the tops of the shells that will hang down from the top of the wreath (see Basic Techniques). Stitch these shells on to the wreath using a darning needle and raffia.

6 Using buttonhole stitch, form a raffia loop at the back of the wreath for hanging.

7 Using a glue gun, stick shells onto the top surface of the wreath, leaving the bottom section undecorated.

8 Stick shells onto the inside and outside surfaces. Fill in the gaps with smaller shells, sticking them on with white glue to avoid the risk of burning your fingers with the glue gun.

9 Stick subtly colored dried flowers on to the wreath with white glue, using them to fill any remaining gaps and to soften the appearance of the wreath.

10 Tie the wide ribbon in a bow and glue it to the top of the wreath.

SCALLOP PLANT TIDY

THIS PLANT TIDY HAS A DOUBLE FUNCTION: IT CAN EITHER BE WRAPPED AROUND A GROUP OF ASSORTED POTTED PLANTS OR HUNG ACROSS A WINDOWSILL TO PREVENT POTS FROM FALLING. IT ALSO HAS THE ADVANTAGE OF NEVER NEEDING REPLANTING; AS BLOSSOMS FADE, SIMPLY REPLACE THE WHOLE POT WITH A MORE SEASONAL PLANT. THE SHELL THEME CAN BE FURTHER EXTENDED TO YOUR GARDEN BY MAKING PRETTY SCALLOP-SHELL EDGINGS AROUND FLOWER BEDS AND BORDERING PATHWAYS OR BY MARKING THE POSITIONS OF PLANTS WITH SCALLOP SHELLS ATTACHED TO THE ENDS OF GARDEN CANES.

1 Measure around the flowerpots to be surrounded with the bamboo screen. Calculate the number of bamboo canes needed to make the screen. Saw lengths of bamboo slightly longer than the height of the flowerpots. Some of the lengths should be about 1½ inches longer.

2 Start binding the bamboo canes together by tying a length of green garden string around the first cane, then looping it around the next.

4 Continue binding the canes together in this way. Bind two longer canes between each group of five shorter canes. (If you are using scallop shells larger than the ones shown here, you will need more shorter canes between the longer ones.) ▶

3 Pass the string under the first loop and between the two canes, then loop it around the second cane again.

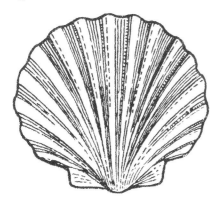

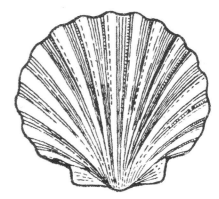

MATERIALS AND EQUIPMENT YOU WILL NEED

TAPE MEASURE • FLOWER POTS • SAW • BAMBOO CANES • GREEN GARDEN STRING • PENCIL • SCALLOP SHELLS • REUSABLE TACKY PUTTY • MINI-DRILL • WIRE-CUTTERS • GALVANIZED GARDEN WIRE • PLIERS

5 When you have finished binding across the bottom of the canes, repeat the process across the top.

7 Secure the shells to the work surface with reusable tacky putty to hold them steady while drilling. Drill the holes from inside the shells (see Basic Techniques).

9 Insert two staples through the holes in each shell. Position the shells on top of the protruding longer canes. Use pliers to twist the wires together at the back to hold the shells in place.

6 With a pencil, mark four points on each shell for drilling.

8 Cut 6-inch lengths of galvanized garden wire and bend the ends up at right angles with pliers to make staples. The width of each staple must be the diagonal distance between the drilled holes. You will need two staples for each shell.

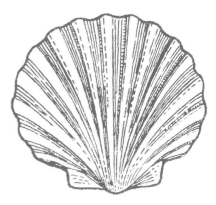

NECKLACE OF SHELLS

SHELLS HAVE BEEN USED SINCE TIME IMMEMORIAL TO DECORATE THE HUMAN FORM. THEY MAKE ALMOST INSTANT ADORNMENT, OFTEN NEEDING JUST A SUITABLE JEWELRY FINDING TO ATTACH THEM TO THE BODY OR CLOTHING. THERE ARE INNUMERABLE WAYS OF MAKING SHELL NECKLACES, AND THIS PROJECT USES ONE OF THE SIMPLEST AND MOST EFFECTIVE METHODS. THE RAINBOW COCKLE SHELLS WITH THEIR PRETTY, VARIEGATED COLORS ARE STITCHED ONTO A COLORED CORD. THE LONG TASSEL LEFT HANGING DOWN AT THE BACK MAKES THE NECKLACE THE PERFECT ACCESSORY FOR BEACHWEAR OR A BACKLESS DRESS.

1 Select an odd number of cockle shells and arrange them around the cord with the largest one in the center at the front.

2 Drill a hole through the top of each shell (see Basic Techniques).

4 Apply instant bonding adhesive to the ends of the cord and insert each end into a small periwinkle shell.

3 Stitch the shells on to the cord using embroidery floss. Choose a color to complement the cord.

MATERIALS AND EQUIPMENT YOU WILL NEED
RAINBOW COCKLE SHELLS • COLORED CORD • REUSABLE TACKY PUTTY • MINI-DRILL • EMBROIDERY FLOSS• EMBROIDERY NEEDLE • INSTANT BONDING ADHESIVE • TWO SMALL PERIWINKLE SHELLS

BEACH-HUT BIRDHOUSE

GIVE THE BIRDS IN YOUR GARDEN A TREAT — A VACATION HOME IN THIS CHARMING BIRD HOUSE BUILT IN THE STYLE OF A BEACH HUT. SHELLS DECORATE THE ENTRANCE AND ACT AS RIDGE TILES ALONG THE ROOF. CUNNING PAINTING TECHNIQUES ARE EMPLOYED TO ACHIEVE THE LOOK OF WEATHERED SEASIDE BUILDINGS. PAINT THE BASE IN THE SAME WAY AS THE HOUSE, BUT USE A DARKER SHADE OF OCHER PAINT. ONCE MADE, THE BIRDHOUSE CAN BE PLACED ON A READY-MADE POST, OR YOU CAN MAKE YOUR OWN. HERE, THE POST HAS BEEN REINFORCED WITH SIDE STRUTS.

1 Following the plans and measurements at the back of the book, cut and glue together four planks of pine for each end piece of the birdhouse, two planks for each side piece and three planks for the table top. Bind each piece firmly together with masking tape.

2 When the glue is dry, remove the masking tape and cut out the gable shapes from the end pieces and the side pieces to size using a saw.

3 Using a spade bit, drill the entrance hole in one end piece. Glue together the four walls. Tape together and let dry.

MATERIALS AND EQUIPMENT YOU WILL NEED

PENCIL • RULER • WORKBENCH • SAW • WOOD GLUE • 5 YARDS OF 2¼ x ½-INCH PINE • MASKING TAPE •
DRILL AND 1¼-INCH SPADE BIT • PANEL PINS • HAMMER • 4½ YARDS OF ¼ x ³⁄₁₆-INCH PINE • CRAFT KNIFE • SANDPAPER •
FRETSAW • WATERCOLOR PAINTS: COBALT BLUE, BURNT UMBER, YELLOW OCHER AND BURNT SIENNA • PAINTBRUSHES •
PETROLEUM JELLY • WHITE LATEX PAINT • BLOW TORCH • TWO PIECES OF ³⁄₁₆-INCH PLYWOOD, EACH 10 x 6½ INCHES •
PIECE OF ROOFING FELT, 15 x 12 INCHES • SMALL NAILS • PLIERS (OPTIONAL) • SCALLOP SHELL • SMALL COCKLE SHELLS •
WHITE GLUE • REUSABLE TACKY PUTTY • MINI-DRILL • SCREWS • SCREWDRIVER

4 Nail together all the seams with panel pins. Add the shelf below the entrance hole by gluing and nailing a ³⁄₁₆-inch strip of pine in position.

6 Lay the strips side by side over each side of the bird house and attach with panel pins.

8 Glue the trim around the table top and nail to secure.

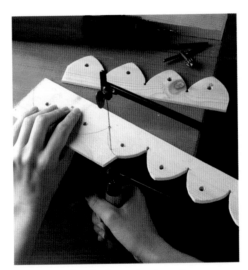

5 Cut the pine strip into lengths to fit the sides of the birdhouse. Round off the edges of each strip by trimming with a craft knife and smoothing with sandpaper.

7 Cut the thicker pine into four lengths to fit the sides of the table top. Following the template at the back of the book, mark the scalloped trim on to the pine. Drill a hole in the center of each scallop, then cut out the trim with a fretsaw.

9 Mix cobalt blue and burnt umber watercolor paints and paint the house and table top with the blue-gray color. Let dry, then rub petroleum jelly all over the surface.

▶

10 Paint over the base coat with white latex paint. Dry with a blow torch so the paint starts to crack and distress; be careful not to burn the paint.

11 Smear diluted ocher and burnt sienna watercolor paint unevenly over the surface to add to the aged appearance.

12 Lay the two pieces of plywood on top of the roofing felt with a gap of approximately ½ inch between them. Turn over the edges of the felt and secure with small nails. You may need to snip the ends off the nails with pliers to make them small enough.

13 Place the roof on the birdhouse and nail in place. Cut four pieces of the pine strip for the roof trim. Paint and distress as in Steps 9–11, using a blue-green color. Nail the trim onto the sides of the roof. Finish with a strip of wood along the top of the roof.

14 Decorate the front of the house by gluing a scallop shell and two cockle shells above the entrance hole with white glue. Drill holes in the small cockle shells (see Basic Techniques) and nail them along the roof ridge. Glue the birdhouse onto the table top with wood glue, and screw in place from underneath.

SNAIL-SHELL BUTTONS

BUTTONS CAN EASILY BE MADE FROM ALL SORTS OF SHELLS, AS LONG AS THERE IS A MEANS OF ATTACHING THEM. THEY LOOK ESPECIALLY EFFECTIVE ON CLOTHING MADE FROM NATURAL FABRICS, SUCH AS WOOL AND COTTON, IN NEUTRAL COLORS. HERE, THE CREVICES IN THE BACKS OF SNAIL SHELLS HAVE BEEN FILLED WITH EPOXY PUTTY, AND EYELET SCREWS HAVE BEEN INSERTED. ONCE THE PUTTY IS DRY, THE BUTTONS CAN BE STITCHED ONTO A GARMENT THROUGH THE EYELET HOLES. IF YOU DO NOT HAVE ENOUGH OF THE SAME TYPE OF SHELL, TRY A COMBINATION OF DIFFERENT SHELLS.

1 Wearing protective gloves, combine the two parts of the epoxy putty. Push putty into the mouth of each snail shell and fill the spiral recesses on the back of the shell. Smooth the surface with your finger.

2 Press a small eyelet screw into the putty on the back of each shell. If the screw is too long, snip off the end with wire-cutters, if using.

3 Let the putty dry, then file or sand smooth, making sure there are no sharp edges at the mouth of the shell. Sew the shell buttons onto the garment with a needle and matching button thread.

MATERIALS AND EQUIPMENT YOU WILL NEED

PROTECTIVE GLOVES • EPOXY PUTTY • SMALL SNAIL SHELLS • SMALL EYELET SCREWS • WIRE-CUTTERS (OPTIONAL) • FILE OR SANDPAPER • NEEDLE • BUTTON THREAD

SCALLOP SCONCE

THE BEAUTY OF THIS PROJECT LIES IN ITS ELEGANT SIMPLICITY; THE LIGHT FROM THE CANDLE RADIATES ALONG THE GROOVES OF THE SHELL, PROVIDING AN ATMOSPHERE OF PEACEFUL SERENITY. THE SCONCE CAN BE USED ON ITS OWN TO LIGHT UP A DARK CORNER OR, FOR A MORE DRAMATIC EFFECT, YOU CAN POSITION SEVERAL SCONCES IN A ROW DOWN A CORRIDOR, ENTRANCE HALL OR EVEN ALONG A SHELTERED GARDEN WALL. TAKE CARE TO POSITION THE SCONCE AWAY FROM FURNITURE AND CURTAINS TO AVOID THE RISK OF FIRE, AND NEVER LEAVE CANDLES BURNING UNATTENDED.

1 Drill a hole on either side of the hinged edge of each scallop shell, just next to the raised part (see Basic Techniques).

3 Wearing protective gloves, mix the two parts of the epoxy putty together. Cover the hinge with putty, working it up to the edge of the raised part of each shell. Poke through the drilled holes with wire to unblock them.

5 Dilute some brown ink with water and paint it over the putty to blend in with the shell.

2 Support the pair of shells on a brick as shown. Use tacky putty to hold them in place. Apply instant bonding adhesive along the hinge.

4 Let putty dry, then sand smooth with a file, sandpaper or a drill with a sanding disc attachment.

6 Thread corded wire through the drilled holes in the shells and bind around and across the hinge as shown. Twist the ends of the wire together with pliers and cut off the excess. Glue the night-light into the sconce.

MATERIALS AND EQUIPMENT YOU WILL NEED

MINI-DRILL • PAIR OF SCALLOP SHELLS • BRICK • REUSABLE TACKY PUTTY • INSTANT BONDING ADHESIVE • PROTECTIVE GLOVES • EPOXY PUTTY • CORDED WIRE • FILE, SANDPAPER OR SANDING DISC FOR DRILL • BROWN INK • PAINTBRUSH • PLIERS • WIRE-CUTTERS • NIGHT-LIGHT

FLOTSAM FAIRY

LEFT HANGING ON AN OUTSIDE WALL OR DOOR, THIS FAIRY CAN PREDICT THE WEATHER, AS HER SEAWEED SKIRT RESPONDS TO THE MOISTURE CONTENT OF THE AIR. ON HOT DAYS, THE SEAWEED WILL BE DRY AND BRITTLE, BUT IF IT BECOMES SOFT AND LEATHERY, BEWARE OF IMMINENT RAIN. THIS IS A LOVELY PROJECT TO MAKE WITH OR FOR A CHILD. CHILDREN WILL LOVE TO COLLECT THE SHELLS AND SEAWEED WHILE ON A BEACH VACATION AND TO TURN THEM INTO THIS MAGICAL DOLL UPON THEIR RETURN. YOU CAN ADAPT THE DESIGN TO SUIT THE TYPES OF SHELLS AND SEAWEED YOU FIND.

1 Drill a hole in one end of each of two razor shells (see Basic Techniques). Slot them between the legs of the "dolly" peg, with the holes at the bottom. Glue them in place for the legs.

2 Arrange one color of seaweed around the peg to make a skirt, securing it in place with an elastic band.

3 Wrap masking tape around the top of the seaweed to create the fairy's torso.

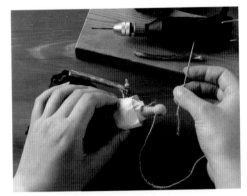

4 Drill a hole through one end of each of two small sticks. Thread a darning needle with string and stitch the sticks onto the doll to make the arms, sewing through the masking tape.

5 Wearing protective gloves, combine the two parts of the epoxy putty and form it into a ball for the fairy's head. Alternatively, you could use modeling clay. Press the head onto the top of the peg.

6 Press a limpet shell onto the front of the head to make the face. ▶

MATERIALS AND EQUIPMENT YOU WILL NEED

MINI-DRILL • REUSABLE TACKY PUTTY • TWO RAZOR SHELLS • WOODEN "DOLLY" PEG • INSTANT BONDING ADHESIVE •
TWO TYPES OF SEAWEED • RUBBER BAND • MASKING TAPE • TWO SMALL STICKS • DARNING NEEDLE • FINE STRING • PROTECTIVE GLOVES •
EPOXY PUTTY OR MODELING CLAY • LIMPET SHELL • RAFFIA: NATURAL, ORANGE AND PINK • TWO BLACK-LIPPED OYSTER SHELLS • TWEEZERS •
TWO BEADS • FOUR COCKLE SHELLS (TWO SMALL, TWO LARGER) • LIP PENCIL • SHELL NECKLACE

7 Wrap natural raffia around the torso to completely cover the masking tape, crossing it over the doll's neck and under the arms.

9 Using instant bonding adhesive and tweezers, stick two beads onto the limpet shell for eyes and two small cockle shells for ears.

11 Drill a hole in each of the larger cockle shells. Using orange raffia and a darning needle, thread and tie them onto the ends of the razor shell legs for shoes. You may also need to glue them into the right position.

8 Drill two holes in each of the two oyster shells. Using a darning needle and string, stitch these onto the back to make wings.

10 Draw lips and cheeks on the limpet shell with a lip pencil. Smudge the cheeks with your fingers.

12 Wrap pink raffia around the fairy's waist. Glue a different color seaweed to the top of the limpet shell to make hair. Tie a pink raffia bow around her hair and add a string of small shells cut from an old necklace.

GROTTO FRAME

IT IS HARD TO BELIEVE THAT THIS BEAUTIFUL, SHELL-ENCRUSTED VISION STARTED LIFE AS A PLAIN WOODEN FRAME. TEXTURE IS BUILT UP USING NEUTRAL-COLORED SHELLS SUCH AS LIMPETS AND COCKLES EMBEDDED RANDOMLY INTO ADHESIVE TILE GROUT. SMALLER, MORE DECORATIVE SHELLS ARE GLUED ONTO THIS BASE TO INTRODUCE COLOR, THEN FROSTED BEADS AND, FINALLY, SPARKLING CLUSTERS OF TINY GLASS BEADS ARE ADDED TO COMPLETE THE GROTTO-LIKE EFFECT. AS THE FRAME HAS A DISTINCT VICTORIAN FEEL, IT IS PARTICULARLY SUITED TO FRAMING POSTCARDS OR TINTED PHOTOGRAPHS FROM THAT ERA.

1 Attach the shells to the frame using white adhesive tile grout and a small palette knife. Let the shells overlap the edges at the top of the frame and its sides to disguise its square shape and to create a grotto-like effect.

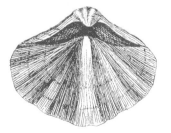

2 Continue to cover the frame around the inside edge, allowing the shells to overlap the edge as before.

3 Fill in the gaps between the shells with smaller shells.

4 Select bumpy shells to cover the side and top edges of the frame; attach them with grout as before. Let the tile grout dry for several hours.

▶

MATERIALS AND EQUIPMENT YOU WILL NEED

ASSORTED SHELLS IN NEUTRAL COLORS • PLAIN WOODEN PICTURE FRAME • WHITE ADHESIVE TILE GROUT • SMALL PALETTE KNIFE •
WHITE GLUE • BLUE LIMPET SHELLS • SMALL COLORED SHELLS • FROSTED GLASS BEADS • TWEEZERS •
SMALL CLEAR GLASS BEADS IN THREE COMPLEMENTARY COLORS • LARGE MATCHSTICK • WHITE LATEX PAINT • PAINTBRUSH • INK (OPTIONAL)

5 Use white glue to stick on decorative blue limpets and small colored shells. These ones have been taken from an old necklace.

6 To add color and texture, glue on frosted glass beads, using tweezers to position them.

7 Mix the clear glass beads into some white glue. Using a large matchstick, blob this mixture into the gaps between the shells on the frame, especially around the inner and outer edges. Let the glue dry.

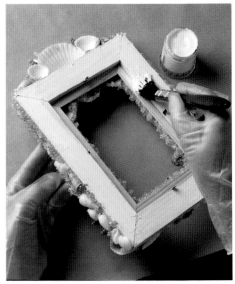

8 Paint the back of the frame with white latex paint. If desired, you can wash over the paint with diluted ink to match your decor.

9 If the frame is free-standing, it is important that the back looks attractive, so finish by attaching a few more shells to the top with tile grout.

SCALLOP-HINGED CUPBOARD

THIS WEATHERED-LOOKING BATHROOM CUPBOARD IS MADE FROM PLANKS OF DRIFTWOOD AND WITTILY USES TWO PAIRS OF SCALLOP SHELLS AS ITS HINGES. THE WINDOW IN THE DOOR CAN BE SCREENED FROM BEHIND WITH AN OLD STRING FISHING NET. THE DOOR WILL REMAIN CLOSED WITHOUT A FASTENING BUT, IF DESIRED, YOU CAN MAKE A HANDLE AS DESCRIBED IN THE DRAWER KNOBS PROJECT. TO MOUNT THE CUPBOARD ON THE WALL, DRILL HOLES THROUGH THE BACK AND SCREW THROUGH THEM FROM THE INSIDE OF THE CUPBOARD INTO MATCHING PLUGGED HOLES DRILLED INTO THE WALL.

1 Saw the planks into nine 20-inch lengths, six 7½-inch lengths and two 8½-inch lengths.

2 Join three 20-inch planks for the back and two pairs of 20-inch planks for the sides by hammering in a corrugated fixer at the top and bottom of each seam. To make the top, bottom and shelf, attach three pairs of 7½-inch planks in the same way.

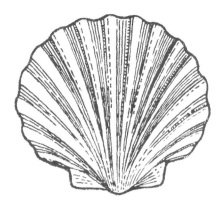

3 Turn each section over and hammer in another corrugated fixer at the center of each seam.

4 To make the door, arrange two 8½-inch planks between two 20-inch planks, as shown. Nail a batten across the planks at the bottom and top of the door. Turn the door over and hammer in a corrugated fixer at the top and bottom of each seam.

5 Position the back on top of the sides and nail together from the back.

MATERIALS AND EQUIPMENT YOU WILL NEED

RULER • PENCIL • WORKBENCH • SAW • PLANKS OF DRIFTWOOD OR WEATHERED WOOD • HAMMER • CORRUGATED FIXERS • 2-INCH NAILS • WOODEN BATTENS • FILE • TWO CONCAVE SCALLOP SHELLS • TWO FLAT SCALLOP SHELLS • TWO BRASS HINGES • REUSABLE TACKY PUTTY • DRILL • EIGHT ¼-INCH BOLTS • NUTS • SCREWDRIVER • TWELVE 1½-INCH BRASS SCREWS

6 Insert the top and bottom panels and nail them to the side panels from the outside. Attach the shelf in the same way.

8 File across the attached edge of each shell so the hinge will lie flush against the shell.

10 Drill through the marked points on each shell, then drill three evenly spaced holes around the curved edge of each shell (see Basic Techniques).

7 File the edges of all the scallop shells to smooth them.

9 Place a hinge over the attached edge of each shell and mark the positions of the holes.

11 Bolt the hinges onto the shells, pairing each concave shell with a flat one. Fix with nuts on the outside. ▶

12 Drill holes around the edge of the cupboard where you want to attach the hinges. Screw the flat half of each pair of shells on to the side of the cupboard through the holes.

13 Screw the concave half of each shell onto the door in the same way.

SHELLY SALAD SERVERS

SCALLOP SHELLS MAKE NATURAL KITCHEN IMPLEMENTS: THE CONCAVE SHAPE PROVIDES A SPOON WHILE THE JAGGED EDGE SERVES AS A KNIFE. UNTIL RECENTLY, THE FLAT HALF OF THE SCALLOP WAS USED ON THE WEST COAST OF IRELAND FOR CHOPPING BOILED CABBAGE. WHEN USING SHELLS FOR CULINARY PURPOSES, IT IS VITAL TO CLEAN THEM THOROUGHLY. SOAK THE SHELLS IN MILD BLEACH OVERNIGHT, THEN SCRUB THE BACKS WITH A WIRE BRUSH. AFTER SEVERAL RINSINGS, POLISH THE SHELLS (SEE BASIC TECHNIQUES). THE WOODEN HANDLES USED HERE ARE TAKEN FROM SCREWDRIVERS.

1 Clean the scallop shells thoroughly (see Basic Techniques) and then soak them in a mild bleach solution. Remove the wings from the shells using a hacksaw.

3 Drill a hole in the tip of each shell large enough to take the bolt shaft (see Basic Techniques).

5 Drill a hole into each wooden handle, making sure it is deep enough to accommodate the full length of the bolt. Thread the bolt through the shell into the handle, taking care not to break the shell as you tighten it. It is a good idea to tighten the bolt into the handle without the shell first to try it out. You can use soap if the bolt is very stiff.

2 File the edges of the shells to make them even and smooth.

4 File the hole square so the coach bolt will fit through it.

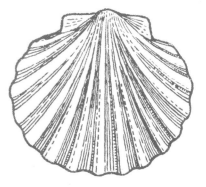

MATERIALS AND EQUIPMENT YOU WILL NEED
TWO SCALLOP SHELLS • BLEACH • HACKSAW • FILE • MINI-DRILL AND GRINDER ATTACHMENT • REUSABLE TACKY PUTTY •
DRILL • TWO COACH BOLTS • TWO WOODEN HANDLES • SOAP (OPTIONAL)

SHORELINE CURTAIN

THE SIMPLE ELEGANCE OF THIS CURTAIN IS EASY TO ACHIEVE BY DRILLING SMALL, LIGHTWEIGHT SHELLS AND STITCHING THEM ONTO A CURTAIN. THE CURTAIN CAN BE MADE FROM FINE MUSLIN, COTTON OR POLYCOTTON FABRIC, WHICH WILL ALLOW DAYLIGHT TO FILTER THROUGH AND CAST THE SHADOWS OF THE SHELLS ONTO THE WALLS AND FLOOR. THE CLOTHESPINS USED INSTEAD OF CURTAIN HOOKS ADD TO THE ROBINSON CRUSOE EFFECT. MANY OF THE SHELLS USED HERE HAVE BEEN RECYCLED FROM OLD, BROKEN NECKLACES. WASH THE CURTAIN CAREFULLY BY HAND WHEN NECESSARY.

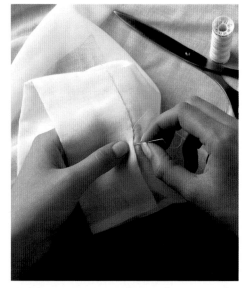

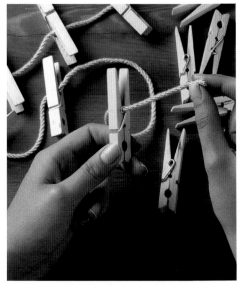

2 Drill a hole in all the shells (see Basic Techniques).

4 Thread wooden clothespins onto a cord through the hole in the spring – the larger the hole, the more easily the curtain will draw back. Attach the cord to your window frame using eyelet screws. Clip the clothespins to the top of the curtain.

1 Measure your window and cut enough fabric to cover it, allowing extra for a slight gather and seams and hems. Make the curtain.

3 Stitch the shells onto the curtain in staggered rows approximately 3 inches apart.

MATERIALS AND EQUIPMENT YOU WILL NEED

TAPE MEASURE • LIGHTWEIGHT COTTON, POLYCOTTON OR MUSLIN FABRIC • SCISSORS • NEEDLE • SEWING THREAD • ASSORTED SMALL SHELLS •
REUSABLE TACKY PUTTY • MINI-DRILL • WOODEN CLOTHESPINS • CORD • EYELET SCREWS

SHELL CHANDELIER

THIS ELEGANT CHANDELIER HOLDS SEVEN CANDLES AND CAN BE USED INDOORS ABOVE A DINNER TABLE OR OUTDOORS FOR A SPECIAL GARDEN PARTY ON A STILL EVENING. IF YOUR SHELLS ARE UNEVEN IN COLOR, YOU COULD SOAK THEM IN A MILD SOLUTION OF BLEACH OVERNIGHT. IT IS IMPORTANT FOR

CHANDELIERS TO HAVE SOME WEIGHT TO GIVE THEM STABILITY, SO THE PERIWINKLE SHELL HANGING AT THE BOTTOM OF THIS ONE IS FILLED WITH EPOXY PUTTY. GLUE THE CANDLE CASES TO THE SHELLS FOR SAFETY AND SIMPLY REPLACE THE WAX CORE AS NECESSARY. NEVER LEAVE CANDLES BURNING UNATTENDED.

1 Position the scallop shells around the baking ring. Mark two points on the hinge edge of each shell, one at each side. Each point should coincide with a channel in the fluting.

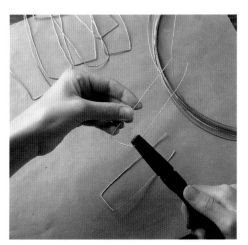

3 Using pliers, make seven staples from the garden wire. Each should be long enough to wrap around the baking ring and as wide as the distance between the holes drilled in two adjoining shells.

4 Wearing protective gloves, mix the two parts of the epoxy putty and roll into sausage shapes. Use to cover the hinge end of each shell.

2 Drill the marked points to make holes large enough to take the galvanized garden wire (see Basic Techniques).

5 Press the edge of the baking ring into the epoxy putty on two of the shells, making sure you line up the holes drilled in the shells with the channels in the fluting. ▶

MATERIALS AND EQUIPMENT YOU WILL NEED

SEVEN SCALLOP SHELLS • FLUTED BAKING RING • BLACK MARKER • REUSABLE TACKY PUTTY • MINI-DRILL •
GALVANIZED GARDEN WIRE • PLIERS • PROTECTIVE GLOVES • EPOXY PUTTY • SCISSORS • WHITE STRING • LARGE PERIWINKLE SHELL •
35 WHITE COCKLE SHELLS IN ASSORTED SIZES • CLEAR GLASS BEADS • PEBBLE WITH A HOLE • EPOXY GLUE • SEVEN CANDLES

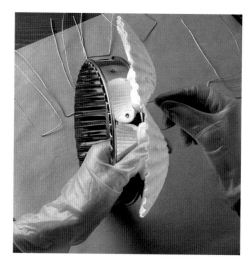

6 Fix the shells in place by inserting a wire staple through the drilled holes in the shells and the channels in the fluting. Leave the ends of wire projecting from the top of the baking ring. Continue adding the shells and staples one at a time.

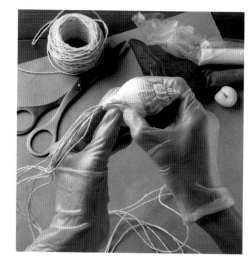

8 Cut seven long lengths of string and insert the ends into the periwinkle shell. Wearing protective gloves, fill the inside of the shell with epoxy putty to secure the strings in place and add weight to the finished chandelier.

10 Knot the end of each string ½ inch above the last shell. Thread a clear glass bead onto each string. The beads should be large enough not to be pulled through the channel in the fluting. Thread the strings up through the channels in the fluting at equal intervals around the ring. Thread another bead onto each string and tie in place so that it rests on the top of the ring.

7 When all the shells are in place, let sit for a couple of hours until the putty is completely dry. Bend the wires over to the outside of the ring and snip off the excess with pliers.

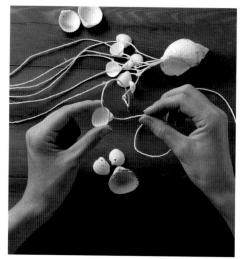

9 Drill a hole in each of the cockle shells and sort them into seven groups of five equally sized shells. Starting with the smallest group, thread a shell onto each string and tie in position. Tie on the rest of the shells at equal intervals along the string and in order of size, finishing with the largest.

11 Gather the strings together at the top and thread them through the hole in the pebble. Knot the strings together and secure with epoxy glue. Glue the candle cases into the shells.

LIMPET LAMP

THIS CONTEMPORARY AND ORIGINAL LAMP IS MADE FROM THICK CANVAS, WHICH IS SELF-SUPPORTING. THE SHADE IS EASY TO MAKE AND CAN BE SLOTTED OVER A ROUND FIBERBOARD OR WOODEN BASE. THE LIMPET SHELLS HAVE SMALL HOLES DRILLED IN THEIR TOPS TO GIVE OFF A SUBTLE GLOW WHEN THE LAMP IS LIT. IT IS ALWAYS IMPORTANT FOR AIR TO BE ABLE TO CIRCULATE INSIDE A LAMPSHADE TO PREVENT OVERHEATING, SO MAKE SURE THERE ARE ENOUGH HOLES AT THE BOTTOM TO ALLOW FOR THIS, AND USE A NARROW COMPACT FLUORESCENT BULB, WHICH DOES NOT GET TOO HOT.

1 Scale up the template from the back of the book onto paper and cut it out. Lay the pattern over the canvas fabric with the selvage at the bottom. Cut around the pattern using a craft knife and metal ruler on a cutting mat.

2 Fold the side and top edges in by ½ inch. Run your finger along each fold, then glue the hems with instant bonding adhesive.

3 Cut a strip of canvas 1½ x 21 inches. Glue it over one of the hems on the inside, so it overlaps the edge by ¾ inch.

4 Drill a hole in the top of each limpet shell (see Basic Techniques), then arrange the limpets over the canvas. Draw around the shells with a pencil or fabric marker and remember which shell goes where. Using a craft knife, cut out a hole inside each drawn outline. ▶

MATERIALS AND EQUIPMENT YOU WILL NEED

PAPER • PENCIL • SCISSORS • STIFF CANVAS FABRIC • CRAFT KNIFE • METAL RULER • CUTTING MAT • INSTANT BONDING ADHESIVE • LIMPET SHELLS • REUSABLE TACKY PUTTY • MINI-DRILL • PIECE OF ¾-INCH MEDIUM-DENSITY FIBERBOARD, 12-INCH SQUARE • JIGSAW • DRILL AND SPADE BIT • SANDPAPER • LAMP FITTING • MASKING TAPE • STAPLES • HAMMER • LOW-HEAT FLUORESCENT LIGHT BULB

5 Glue the shells in their correct positions over the holes, pressing around the rim from behind.

6 Spread glue along the overlapping strip of canvas and attach it to the opposite edge of the canvas. Insert your arm into the cone and run your fingers firmly down the seam to secure.

7 Cut a circular base 11 inches in diameter from the fiberboard using a jigsaw. Using the spade bit, drill a hole through the center large enough to hold the lamp fitting. Sand the edges of the base smooth.

8 Wrap masking tape around the bottom of the lamp fitting to ensure a snug fit and insert it into the hole in the base.

9 Attach the flex to the top and side of the base by hammering staples over it.

10 Place a low-heat fluorescent light bulb in the lamp fitting. Insert the canvas shade over the base; it should be a tight fit.

ROCK-POOL FOUNTAIN

SHELLS ARE A NATURAL CHOICE FOR A WATER FEATURE. HERE, WATER POURS FROM THE MOUTH OF A LARGE SNAIL SHELL INTO A SERIES OF SCALLOP SHELLS TO CREATE A WATERFALL THAT FLOWS INTO A LARGE EARTHENWARE POT. THE WATER IS PUMPED BACK UP AND THROUGH A HOLE IN THE BACK OF THE SNAIL SHELL. SUITABLE POTTED PLANTS ARE PLACED AROUND THE FOUNTAIN FOR A LOVELY LEAFY EFFECT, AND DECORATIVE SHELLS ARE ARRANGED AROUND THE POT. POSITION THE FOUNTAIN IN A SHADY CORNER OF YOUR GARDEN TO PROVIDE A RESTFUL SPOT IN WHICH TO RELAX AWAY FROM THE HOT SUMMER SUN.

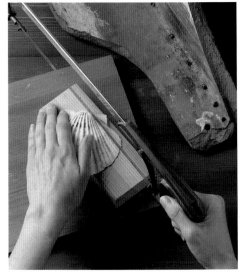

1 Paint the galvanized metal tub with red oxide paint and let dry.

2 Arrange the scallop shells in a tier, with the largest shell at the base, inside the hip tile, and mark their positions. Drill a hole at each mark along the inside bend of the hip tile. Drill an extra hole next to the top hole. Fit all the holes with wall plugs except for the last one drilled.

3 Cut the end of the first scallop shell into a right angle with a hacksaw so it will fit inside the hip tile. File the edges as necessary.

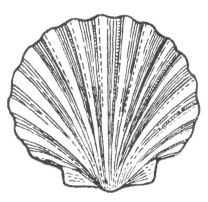

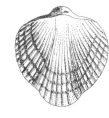

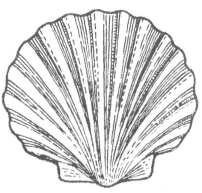

MATERIALS AND EQUIPMENT YOU WILL NEED

GALVANIZED METAL TUB • RED OXIDE PAINT • PAINTBRUSH • FIVE SCALLOP SHELLS IN DIFFERENT SIZES • OLD, BROKEN HIP TILE OR SIMILAR • MARKER • DRILL • WORKBENCH • WALL PLUGS • HACKSAW • FILE • REUSABLE TACKY PUTTY • MINI-DRILL • BRASS SCREWS • SCREWDRIVER • LARGE SNAIL SHELL • ROUND FILE • SMALL PUMP • FINE GARDEN WIRE • PLIERS • RUBBER POND-LINER • WATERPROOF CERAMIC POT • SPONGE (OPTIONAL) • BROKEN TILES OR STONES • ASSORTED SHELLS • SCISSORS • POTTED PLANTS (OPTIONAL) • FINE GRAVEL (OPTIONAL) • BOLT • SMALL WALL PLANTER

4 Drill a hole in the tip of the shell (see Basic Techniques) and screw it into the first hole in the hip tile.

6 Drill a hole in the back of the large snail shell (see Basic Techniques), taking care not to drill right through to the other side of the shell.

8 Fix the snail shell onto the top of the hip tile with fine garden wire, looping the wire under the top scallop shell and twisting the ends together with pliers to secure.

5 Repeat Steps 3–4 with all the shells, attaching them in order of size with the largest at the bottom and the smallest at the top.

7 Enlarge the hole with a round file until it is big enough to take the pump hose, then insert the pump hose in the hole.

9 Line the inside of the tub with the rubber pond-liner. ▶

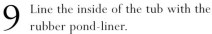

10 Place a waterproof ceramic pot inside the tub, underneath the bottom scallop.

12 Lay shells around the top of the tub. Trim off the excess pond-liner with scissors.

14 Sprinkle some fine gravel over the shells, if desired. Bolt a small wall planter onto the hip tile through the extra hole drilled at the top, and plant it with a trailing plant.

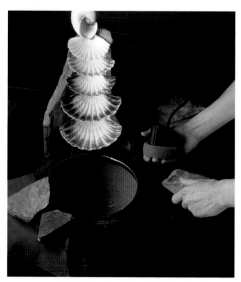

11 Place the pump at the back of the tile, surrounding it with sponge to act as a filler, if desired. Make sure the pump is hidden but easily accessible. Fill the tub with broken tiles or stones.

13 Place potted, water-loving plants in the tub, if desired, for a softer decorative effect.

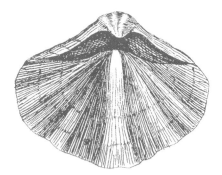

DRIFTWOOD MIRROR

SEARCHING FOR DRIFTWOOD IS A PLEASURE IN ITSELF, AS IT IS OFTEN SCULPT-ED BY THE SEA INTO WONDERFUL SHAPES. THE PIECES YOU FIND MIGHT SHOW THE FADED REMNANTS OF PAINTWORK OR LETTERING. HERE, PIECES OF DRIFT-WOOD HAVE BEEN ASSEMBLED TO MAKE A MIRROR FRAME; TRY TO FIND AN OLD,

WORN MIRROR, WHICH WILL COMPLEMENT THE WOOD BETTER THAN A SHINY NEW ONE. THE LIMPET SHELLS PROVIDE THE FINISHING TOUCH AND ARE EVOCATIVE OF BARNACLE-ENCRUSTED FISHING BOATS. FILL IN THE GAPS BETWEEN THE MIRROR AND FRAME WITH SMALL PIECES OF DRIFTWOOD, SPONGE OR SEAWEED.

1 Arrange four pieces of driftwood to make a pleasing frame shape.

3 Attach the mirror onto the backing board using mirror corners.

5 Screw mirror plates onto the back and attach a cord for hanging.

2 Saw four pieces of wood to make a backing board slightly smaller than the frame. Screw the backing board together with two screws at each corner. You may need to drill holes for the screws first.

4 Screw the backing board onto the frame pieces from the back using long screws.

6 Glue weathered limpet shells randomly around the frame using white glue.

MATERIALS AND EQUIPMENT YOU WILL NEED

LARGE PIECES OF DRIFTWOOD • SAW • WORKBENCH • ASSORTED SCREWS • SCREWDRIVER • DRILL (OPTIONAL) • MIRROR •
FOUR MIRROR CORNERS • TWO MIRROR PLATES • CORD • WEATHERED LIMPET SHELLS • WHITE GLUE

SEASIDE HAT

THE PERFECT SEASIDE ACCESSORY FOR CHILDREN PLAYING ON THE BEACH, THIS HAT WILL PROVIDE PROTECTION FROM THE SUN AND LOOK GREAT AT THE SAME TIME. THE STITCHES USED TO DECORATE THE HAT ARE SO SIMPLE THAT A CHILD WOULD ENJOY HELPING YOU. WHY NOT MAKE YOURSELF ONE TO MATCH, WHILE YOU ARE AT IT? YOU COULD ALSO STITCH SHELLS ONTO A BEACH BAG AND ESPADRILLES FOR A COORDINATED BEACH LOOK.

1 Using a darning needle and blue string, backstitch around the base of the hat's brim.

3 Using a double thickness of rust embroidery floss, work large, evenly spaced cross-stitches around the brim.

4 Drill a hole in the tip of each cockle shell (see Basic Techniques), and stitch one between each pair of cross-stitches using light green embroidery floss.

2 Blanket stitch evenly around the top of the brim with blue string.

5 Wrap a ribbon around the crown of the hat and hold in place with just a few stitches here and there.

MATERIALS AND EQUIPMENT YOU WILL NEED

DARNING NEEDLE • FINE BLUE STRING • RAFFIA OR STRAW HAT WITH TURN-UP BRIM • SCISSORS • EMBROIDERY FLOSS: RUST AND LIGHT GREEN • WHITE COCKLE SHELLS • REUSABLE TACKY PUTTY • MINI-DRILL • RIBBON • SEWING NEEDLE AND THREAD

VACATION ALBUM

Make an album to capture the ambience of your seaside vacation with shells, raffia matting and postcards. The cover of this album is made from polyboard and the pages from recycled cardboard, bound together with raffia to fit the natural theme. Books of this type tend to bulge when they are full, so tie a ribbon in seaside colors around the finished album to prevent your photographs from falling out.

1 Using a craft knife, metal ruler and a cutting mat, cut a rectangle of polyboard 24 x 8½ inches. Mark the center line across the width of the polyboard on both sides. Mark a parallel line ¼ inch from each side of the center line. Partially cut through the board along these two lines, taking great care not to cut through the full thickness of the polyboard. This 1½-inch strip will form the book's spine.

2 Turn the board over and stick double-sided carpet tape around all the edges. Mark a line 2⅛ inches from each side of the center line. Partially cut through the board along these two lines as before.

3 Fold the polyboard along the cut lines to form the spine and hinges of the book. Using a bradawl, pierce holes along both hinges 2¼ inches in from the top and bottom edges, and at ¾-inch intervals between these holes.

4 Cut a piece of raffia matting large enough to cover the polyboard and overlap the edges. Lay the board on top of the matting and remove the paper backing from the double-sided carpet tape. Fold the matting around the board and stick the edges to the double-sided tape. Miter the corners neatly. ▶

MATERIALS AND EQUIPMENT YOU WILL NEED

CRAFT KNIFE • METAL RULER • CUTTING MAT • POLYBOARD • PENCIL • DOUBLE-SIDED CARPET TAPE • BRADAWL • SCISSORS •
FINE RAFFIA MATTING • PINS • DARNING NEEDLE • RUST-COLORED RAFFIA • THIN RECYCLED CARDBOARD • TISSUE PAPER • TABLE KNIFE •
GLUE STICK • HOLE PUNCH • POSTCARDS OR PHOTOS • ASSORTED SHELLS • WHITE GLUE • RIBBON

5 Cut another piece of matting to line the inside, allowing for a small hem. Lay it on top of the inside of the board, fold the edges under and pin in place. Thread a darning needle with raffia and overstitch all around the outside edge. Stitch through both layers of matting but not through the polyboard.

6 Cut 20 sheets of thin recycled cardboard 12¼ x 7¼ inches to make the pages of the photo album. Cut 20 sheets of tissue paper 11 x 7 inches. Using a table knife, score two lines, one 1¼ inches and another 1½ inches from one short edge of each piece of cardboard.

7 Fold each piece of cardboard along the first scored line. Run the glue stick inside the fold and insert a piece of tissue paper. Press firmly to seal.

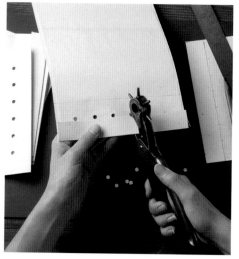

8 Using a hole punch, make holes just above the folded edge and 1¼ inches from the top and bottom edges, and at ¾-inch intervals between these holes.

9 Pile the pages on top of each other and place them inside the cover. Using the darning needle and raffia, stitch the pages to the cover through the punched holes, making a criss-cross pattern down the spine.

10 Decorate the front of the album with old postcards or photos and shells, sticking them in place with white glue. Finally, tie a piece of ribbon around the album to add the finishing touch.

SEAWORN MOBILE

THIS DELICATE MOBILE CAN BE USED AS A WALL HANGING OR AS A WIND CHIME: WHEN IT IS HUNG IN THE BREEZE, ITS TINKLING SOUND IS REMINISCENT OF THE SEA AND IS VERY PLEASANT TO LISTEN TO. THE STONE-EFFECT BEADS USED HERE COME IN A RANGE OF SMOOTH SHAPES AND NATURAL COLORS. REAL PEBBLES THAT HAVE WEATHERED HOLES IN THEM CAN ALSO BE USED, AS LONG AS THEY ARE NOT TOO HEAVY AND ALLOW THE MOBILE TO MOVE IN THE BREEZE.

1 To make the frame, select two pieces of driftwood each about 14 inches long, and drill a hole through either end of each piece.

2 Cut two 22-inch lengths of rough string and knot a long, thin stone-effect bead onto either end of each length, leaving enough string at the ends to thread through the driftwood.

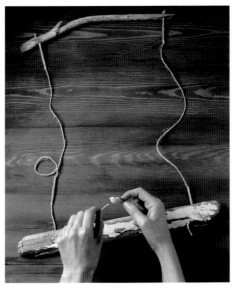

3 Thread one end of each piece of string through the hole in the piece of driftwood for the top of the frame and secure with a knot. Thread the other end through the hole in the bottom piece of wood. Thread a small cockle shell onto the end of each piece of string and secure with a knot.

4 To make the limpet wind chime, mark six points about ¾ inches apart along the length of a small driftwood stick. Drill a hole at each point.

5 Cut six 15-inch lengths of rough string. Thread and tie the limpet shells along each length. Thread the strings through the holes in the driftwood stick and secure with a knot. Cut off any excess string. ▶

MATERIALS AND EQUIPMENT YOU WILL NEED

ASSORTED PIECES OF DRIFTWOOD • DRILL • REUSABLE TACKY PUTTY • MINI-DRILL • SCISSORS • ROUGH STRING • ASSORTED STONE-EFFECT BEADS • TWO COCKLE SHELLS • RULER • PENCIL • WEATHERED LIMPET SHELLS • NATURAL RAFFIA • FIVE CONCH SHELLS • INSTANT BONDING ADHESIVE • LARGE PERIWINKLE SHELL • STICKY TAPE

6 To make the tailed periwinkle shell, cut short lengths of raffia. Glue four or five lengths into the mouth of each conch shell with instant bonding adhesive.

8 Braid three long strands of raffia together and bind one end of the braid with sticky tape to make a point. Thread this end through the hole drilled in the periwinkle shell. Tie the end in a knot and pull the knot inside the shell.

10 Thread stone-effect beads and small pieces of driftwood onto the raffia braid, tying them in position at intervals along the length.

7 Drill a hole in the top tip of the large periwinkle shell (see Basic Techniques).

9 Gather the conch shells and glue the ends of their raffia tails inside the mouth of the periwinkle shell with instant bonding adhesive, so the shells hang down like a tail.

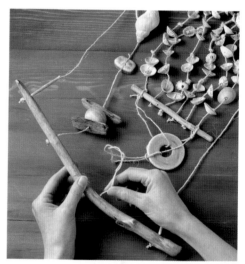

11 To assemble, drill two holes through the top of the frame. Attach the tailed periwinkle shell by threading the end of the raffia braid through one of the holes and secure with a knot. Tie a doubled length of string to each end of the top of the limpet wind chime. Tie both strings around a large, round stone-effect bead, then thread the ends through the second hole in the top of the frame, and knot.

PLAYHOUSE BY THE SEA

IF YOU ARE SKILLED AT DO-IT-YOURSELF WORK, YOU CAN MAKE YOUR CHILD'S DREAM COME TRUE WITH THIS ENCHANTING PLAYHOUSE. IF THE PROJECT SEEMS TOO AMBITIOUS, TRY ADAPTING THE ROOF OF YOUR SHED, PORCH OR EVEN A DOG KENNEL. FLAT SCALLOP SHELLS MAKE NATURAL TILES, AS LONG AS YOU OVERLAP THEM ENOUGH SO THE WATER RUNS DOWN THROUGH THE GROOVES. SCALLOP SHELLS ARE THROWN AWAY BY SEAFOOD RESTAURANTS ALL THE TIME, SO MAKE FRIENDS WITH YOUR LOCAL RESTAURANT OWNERS AND SEE IF THEY WILL KEEP SOME FOR YOU. ALTERNATIVELY, TRY YOUR LOCAL FISH SUPPLIER.

1 Mark out and cut out all the pieces for the playhouse following the diagrams at the back of the book. Use a jigsaw to cut the stirling board. Cut out all the doors and windows, reserving the removed pieces. Cut out the turret pieces.

2 Referring to the diagram at the back of the book, arrange the thicker window pane struts into a cross shape. Lay the plastic sheet on top of this. Arrange the smaller struts in a cross on top and drill pilot holes for screws through all three layers. Position the larger window pane cross and the plastic sheet behind the front window opening.

3 Slot the smaller cross into the window opening. Screw the window together from the front through the pilot holes. Screw through the stirling board and the edges of the plastic into the struts of the larger window pane cross at the back. Cut the square of stirling board from the window in half to make two shutters, and attach them to the side window frame pieces with two 2½-inch hinges on each. Screw the side window frame pieces on either side of the window, then complete by screwing on the top and bottom window frame pieces from the back.

MATERIALS AND EQUIPMENT YOU WILL NEED

FRAMEWORK – FOUR SHEETS STIRLING BOARD, 8 X 4 FEET • WOOD: 43¾ X ¾ X ¾ INCHES AND 35 X ¾ X ¾ INCHES FOR WINDOW PANE STRUTS; 79 X 1⅔ X ½ INCHES FOR WINDOW FRAME; 45 X 2¾ X ¾ INCHES FOR DOOR JAMB; 45 X 1¾ X ½ INCHES FOR DOOR POST; FOUR LENGTHS 45 X 1¾ X 1¾ INCHES FOR CORNER POSTS; 60 X ¾ X ¾ INCHES FOR ROOF BEAM; ELEVEN LENGTHS 35 X 5½ X ½ INCHES FOR FLOORBOARDS; FOUR LENGTHS 23½ X 1¼ X 1¼ INCHES FOR ROOF BATTENS; FOUR LENGTHS 4¾ X ¾ X ¾ INCHES FOR RIDGE BATTENS • PRESSURE-TREATED TIMBER: THREE LENGTHS 60 X 4 X 1¾ INCHES FOR FLOOR JOISTS •

PENCIL • RULER • JIGSAW • WORKBENCH • SAW • CLEAR SHEET OF PLASTIC, 20 X 16 INCHES • DRILL • SCREWS • SCREWDRIVER • SIX 2½-INCH HINGES • TWO SMALL BOLTS • 1-INCH ROOFING BOLTS • SUFFOLK LATCH • FOUR 2¾-INCH HINGES • ASSORTED NAILS • HAMMER • ROOFING FELT • CRAFT KNIFE • 400 FLAT SCALLOP SHELLS • MINI-DRILL • REUSABLE TACKY PUTTY • THREE 2-INCH ANGLE BRACKETS • ALUMINUM ROOFING TAPE • PRIMER • UNDERCOAT • PAINT • PAINTBRUSHES

4 Make a single shutter with the piece of stirling board cut from the side window by attaching it with two 2½-inch hinges directly onto the side panel. Attach a small bolt to the shutter so it can be closed. No frame or window pane is required for this window. Join each side panel to a gable triangle by placing a backing board behind the seam and bolting the pieces together with roofing bolts.

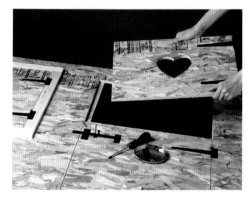

5 Cut the removed door section into two pieces, following the measurements at the back of the book. Cut out the heart motif from the top section with a jigsaw. Attach the door jamb piece to the inside of the door opening so that it overlaps the opening by about ¾ inch. Screw the Suffolk latch onto the lower door section and the 2¾-inch hinges onto the upper and lower door sections. Place the door post

piece behind the wall panel and screw the hinges into the post through the panel. Attach a small bolt to hold the two parts of the door together from the inside.

6 Screw a treated timber floor joist along the inside bottom edge of both the front and back panels. Screw the corner posts to the inside side edges of the front and back panels, leaving a gap of ½ inch between the floor joist and the bottom of the posts, so the floorboards can be slotted in.

7 Prop up the wall panels and screw the side panels into the corner posts.

8 Position the roof beam between the gables at the top. Screw through from the outside wall to secure the roof beam in place.

9 Place the third floor joist centrally between the first two and screw it in place through the outside walls. Lay the floorboards side by side over the joists, slotting them between the joists and the corner posts at the ends of the house, and nail them down. ▶

10 To make the roof, screw two roof battens on to the inside of each roof panel. Attach each batten 6 inches in from the side edge and centrally between the top and bottom edges. Place each roof panel on top of the roofing felt and cut the felt with a craft knife and ruler, allowing for an overlap all the way around the edge.

11 Turn over the edges of the felt and nail them down with small nails.

12 Attach the roof to the house by screwing through the gable from the outside into the roof battens.

13 Drill a hole at the top of each scallop shell. Saw the shells for the ends of every alternate row in half (see Basic Techniques). Nail the shells onto the roof, starting at the bottom and with each row overlapping the previous row like roofing tiles.

14 Assemble the roof ridge pieces with a turret piece at each end. Place the ridge battens inside the seams at the ends and screw from the outside into the ridge batten pieces. Reinforce the roof ridge with three evenly spaced angle brackets.

15 Run a strip of aluminum roofing tape along the ridge join. Drill a hole in each turret and bolt a pair of scallop shells to each turret. Finally, paint the playhouse in the colors of your choice. If it is to be kept outside, ensure that you use exterior-grade paint.

ROPE AND SHELL TASSELS

TASSELS ARE EXPENSIVE TO BUY AND IT IS OFTEN HARD TO FIND ONE THAT WILL FIT IN WITH A NATURAL-STYLE DECOR. THESE SHELL-DECORATED TASSELS ARE EASY AND INEXPENSIVE TO MAKE. THE LARGEST IS MADE FROM A WOODEN MOP HEAD AND THE SMALLER ONES FROM ROPE GLUED INSIDE SHELLS.

WHEN COTTON ROPE IS UNRAVELED AND COMBED, IT MAKES LOVELY SOFT AND WAVY TASSELS, WHICH CAN BE USED TO TIE BACK CURTAINS OR AS LIGHT PULLS. WHEN CUTTING COTTON ROPE, TAPE IT FIRMLY FIRST AND CUT THROUGH THE TAPE TO PREVENT THE ROPE FROM UNRAVELING AS YOU WORK WITH IT.

1 To make the large tassel, paint the wooden mop head with diluted white latex paint.

2 Cut a length of thick cotton rope with a craft knife, binding the ends with masking tape. Use a glue gun to glue it into the hole made for the mop handle.

3 Glue the periwinkle shells onto strands of the mop, spacing them evenly around the mop head.

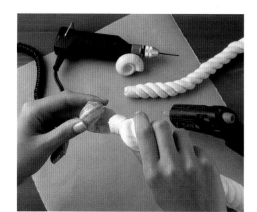

4 To make each small tassel, drill a hole in the side of a snail shell opposite the shell's mouth (see Basic Techniques). Knot the end of a strand of raffia, thread it

through the mouth of the shell and out through the drilled hole. Form it into a small loop. Cut a length of thick rope as before and glue one end inside the mouth of the shell.

5 Cut the rope to the required length of the tassel, unravel it and comb it out. Thread a length of thinner rope through the raffia loop at the top of the shell. Thread a pebble onto the rope, tuck the end of the rope into the hole in the pebble and glue it in place.

MATERIALS AND EQUIPMENT YOU WILL NEED

WOODEN MOP HEAD • WHITE LATEX PAINT • PAINTBRUSH • CRAFT KNIFE • THICK AND THIN COTTON ROPE • MASKING TAPE • GLUE GUN AND GLUE STICKS • FOUR LARGE, WEATHERED PERIWINKLE SHELLS • TWO SNAIL SHELLS • REUSABLE TACKY PUTTY • MINI-DRILL • NATURAL RAFFIA • COMB • TWO PEBBLES WITH HOLES THROUGH THE MIDDLE

VALENTINE'S LOCKET

TRADITION HAS IT THAT SAILORS SENT HOME VALENTINE'S GIFTS MADE FROM SHELLS TO THEIR LOVED ONES. THE SHELL USED TO MAKE THIS ROMANTIC LOCKET IS CALLED A HEART COCKLE BECAUSE OF ITS PERFECT HEART SHAPE. IT OPENS NATURALLY DOWN THE MIDDLE, REVEALING A CHAMBER LARGE ENOUGH TO CONCEAL A MESSAGE OR SMALL MEMENTO. HERE, THE WORDS "I LOVE YOU" HAVE BEEN EMBROIDERED ONTO A PLEATED RIBBON GLUED INSIDE THE SHELL. THE RIBBON NECKLACE IS LOOPED AROUND THE SHELL TO HOLD IT CLOSED. MEMENTOES COULD INCLUDE A LOCK OF HAIR, A TINY BOUQUET OR A PHOTOGRAPH.

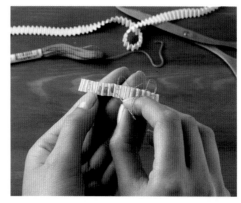

2 Using pink embroidery floss and an embroidery needle, stitch the words "I love you" inside the pleats of a small piece of pleated satin ribbon.

1 Holding the shell steady on a piece of reusable tacky putty, drill a small hole through the top of each half (see Basic Techniques).

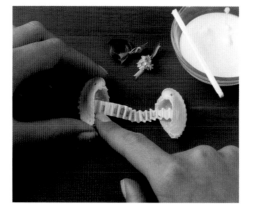

4 Thread a fine silk ribbon through the holes at the top of the shell and wrap it around the shell to hold it closed.

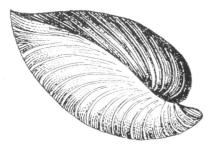

3 Glue the ends of the ribbon inside the halves of the cockle shell and let dry. Close the shell, tucking the ribbon inside and inserting small mementoes.

MATERIALS AND EQUIPMENT YOU WILL NEED

HEART COCKLE SHELL • REUSABLE TACKY PUTTY • WOODEN BLOCK • MINI-DRILL • PINK EMBROIDERY FLOSS • EMBROIDERY NEEDLE •
PLEATED SATIN RIBBON • SCISSORS • WHITE GLUE • SMALL MEMENTOES • FINE SILK RIBBON

SANDCASTLE CLOCK

REFERENCES TO THE SEA ARE VERY FITTING WHEN MAKING A CLOCK. HERE, THE CONSTANT FLOW OF TIME IS MARKED WITH SHELLS, AND THE CLOCK FACE IS COVERED WITH SAND. THE CLOCK REFLECTS THE ARCHITECTURE OF THE SEASIDE: PIERS, PROMENADES, BEACH HUTS AND SANDCASTLES CAN ALL BE GLIMPSED IN THE STRUCTURE. CHILDREN'S BUILDING BLOCKS FORM THE BASE OF THE CLOCK AND, AS THEY ARE ALREADY FINISHED, THEY TAKE THE HARD WORK OUT OF THE PROJECT. SIMPLY COLOR IN THE BLOCKS WITH BLUE AND WHITE WATER-BASED CRAYONS AND THE REST IS CHILD'S PLAY!

1 Refer to the picture of the finished clock to select the building blocks you will need for each part of the clock, or adapt the design as needed. Using crayons, roughly color some blocks blue and some white with long strokes.

2 Glue together the pieces to make the clock's base using wood glue, and measure and mark the positions of the uprights and the top turret on the top. The clock mechanism should fit between them.

3 Glue the uprights in position, assemble the top turret and let dry. Glue the top turret onto the uprights and let dry.

4 Glue together the appropriate blocks to make the side turrets. Glue them onto the base and let the glue dry. Brush over the crayon on all the pieces with a wet paintbrush to give a washed-out effect. You may want to add more color in places. ▶

MATERIALS AND EQUIPMENT YOU WILL NEED

PLAIN WOODEN BUILDING BLOCKS • WATER-BASED CRAYONS: BLUE AND WHITE • WOOD GLUE • RULER • PENCIL • PAINTBRUSH • POLYBOARD • SANDPAPER • CRAFT KNIFE • METAL RULER • CUTTING MAT • DOUBLE-SIDED CARPET TAPE • COMPASS • SCALPEL • WHITE GLUE • SAND • THIN CARDBOARD • SET SQUARE OR PROTRACTOR • PIN • TWELVE SMALL AND TWO LARGE WHITE COCKLE SHELLS • PAPER • TOOTHPICK • BATTERY-OPERATED CLOCK MECHANISM AND HANDS • DECORATIVE FOIL • TWO SMALL MODEL BIRDS (OPTIONAL)

5 To make the clock face, cut a
4½ x 4½ inch square from polyboard
and one from sandpaper using a craft knife
and a metal ruler on a cutting mat. Cover
one side of the polyboard with double-
sided carpet tape. Remove the backing
paper and stick the sandpaper onto it.

6 Using a compass, draw a small circle
in the center of the square and cut
it out carefully using a scalpel. Spread
white glue over the surface and around the
edges of the sandpaper and dip it into
some sand.

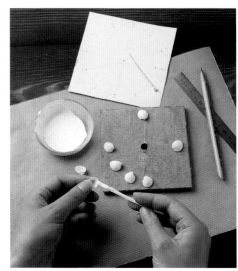

7 Cut a square of cardboard the same
size as the clock face. Using a
compass and a pencil, draw a circle on the
cardboard slightly smaller than the
cardboard. Using a set square or protractor,
divide the circle into twelve 30 degree
segments. Mark the point where each line
meets the edge of the circle. Position the
cardboard over the clock face and prick
through each point with a pin. Glue a
small cockle shell on each pin mark.

8 Cut out and color a small paper flag
and glue it onto a toothpick. Trim
the hands so they will rotate inside the
circle of cockle shells, and cover them
with foil.

9 Glue a large cockle shell onto the
front of each upright. Glue the clock
face onto the front of the castle.

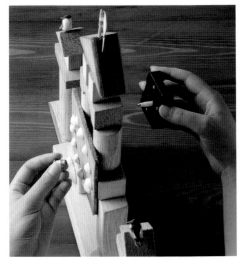

10 Glue a small model bird onto
the top of each side turret, if
desired. Attach the clock mechanism by
inserting the pivotal pin through the hole
from behind and screwing on the nut at
the front.

MOSAIC TABLE

THIS SIMPLE CHIPBOARD TABLE TOP HAS BEEN TRANSFORMED WITH A SHELL MOSAIC INTO A LOVELY PIECE OF FURNITURE, PERFECT FOR A PATIO OR CONSERVATORY. USING A MIXTURE OF MUSSELS, SCALLOPS, A SEA URCHIN AND SMALLER SHELLS FROM OLD NECKLACES, A PATTERN HAS BEEN BUILT UP AROUND A STARFISH MOTIF IN THE CENTER. IT IS A GOOD IDEA TO PRACTICE THE MOSAIC TECHNIQUE ON SOME OLD FLOWERPOTS BEFORE STARTING ON THE TABLE TOP. SYMMETRICAL PATTERNS WORK BEST, SO MAKE SURE YOU HAVE ENOUGH OF EACH TYPE OF SHELL TO GO ALL THE WAY AROUND THE TABLE TOP BEFORE YOU START.

1 Using a ruler, pencil, protractor and a compass, draw a geometric pattern on the table top, following the one shown here or your own design.

2 Using white glue, stick a scallop shell to the center of the table. Glue pink shell pieces from an old necklace inside the starfish shape and surround the starfish with a circle of small snail shells.

3 Break up a sea urchin into mosaic-sized pieces using tile nippers, and glue in a circle outside the snail shells.

4 Glue ten scallop shells around the edge of the table top, spacing them evenly. Fill in the gaps between the scallop shells with mussel shells. Glue cowrie shells in arches between the scallops. ▶

MATERIALS AND EQUIPMENT YOU WILL NEED

RULER • PENCIL • PROTRACTOR • COMPASS • ROUND CHIPBOARD TABLE, APPROXIMATELY 20 INCHES IN DIAMETER • WHITE GLUE • CORAL-COLORED SCALLOP SHELLS (CLEANED AND SANDED) • ASSORTMENT OF SHELLS FROM OLD NECKLACES (SHELL PIECES, SNAILS, COCKLES, COWRIES, ETC.)• SEA URCHIN • TILE NIPPERS • MUSSEL SHELLS (CLEANED AND SANDED) • LIMPET SHELLS (CLEANED AND SANDED) • WHITE ADHESIVE TILE GROUT • GROUT SPREADER OR SMALL PALETTE KNIFE • PAINTBRUSHES • OLD PIECE OF FLANNEL • DRILL AND MOP ATTACHMENT OR SOFT CLOTH • WATER-BASED PAINTS: PALE BLUE-GREEN AND PALE OCHER

5 Glue a limpet shell in the middle of each space in the inner circle. Fill in the spaces around the starfish with small cockle shells.

7 Starting in the center and working on only a small area at a time, spread adhesive tile grout over the surface of the mosaic. Use a grout spreader or palette knife to press the grout into the gaps.

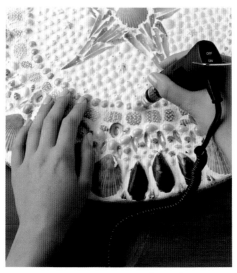

9 Repeat Steps 7–8 until you have grouted the whole mosaic. Leave to dry for several hours, then polish with a mop attachment on your drill or with a soft cloth.

6 Fill in the remaining spaces on the table top with an assortment of small shells arranged in a regular pattern.

8 Use a paintbrush to work the grout into the gaps and smooth the surface with a little water. Press firmly with a damp piece of flannel to impact the grout around the shells. Rub the flannel over the shells in an outward direction to remove any grout from the surface of the shells.

10 Paint the grouting with diluted latex or watercolor paints: pale blue-green for the inner circle and outer edge, and pale ocher for the middle band. Finally, apply several coats of pale blue-green colorwash to the edge of the table top.

PLANS AND TEMPLATES

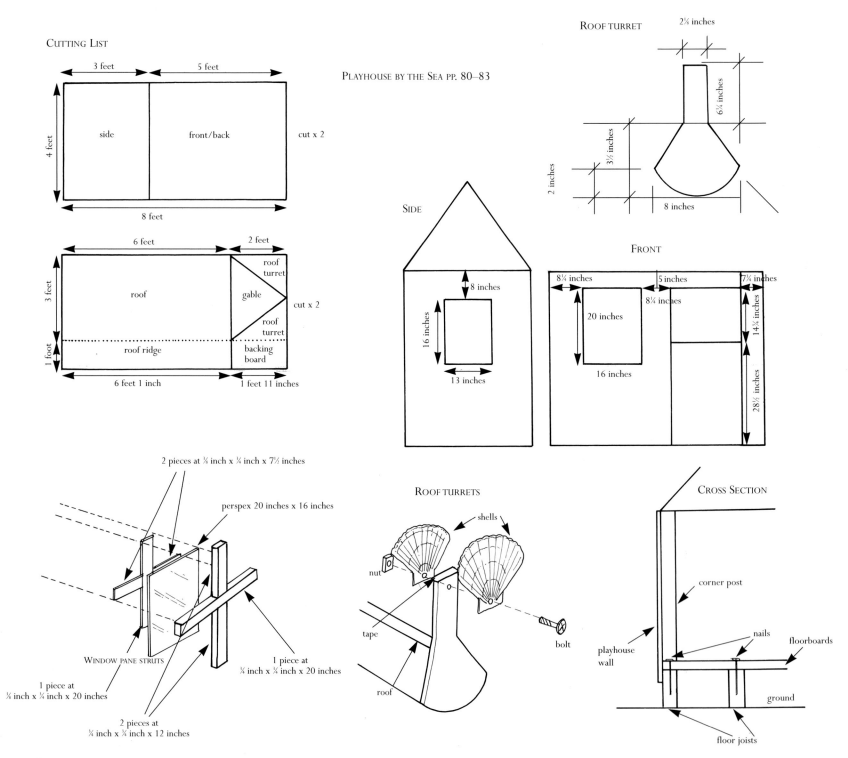

CUTTING LIST

3 feet · 5 feet

4 feet

side · front/back · cut x 2

8 feet

PLAYHOUSE BY THE SEA PP. 80–83

ROOF TURRET

2⅛ inches

6¼ inches

3½ inches

2 inches

8 inches

6 feet · 2 feet

3 feet

roof · gable · roof turret · cut x 2

roof turret

1 foot

roof ridge · backing board

6 feet 1 inch · 1 feet 11 inches

SIDE

8 inches

16 inches

13 inches

FRONT

8¼ inches · 5 inches · 7¼ inches

8¼ inches

20 inches

14¼ inches

16 inches

28½ inches

2 pieces at ⅛ inch x ¼ inch x 7½ inches

perspex 20 inches x 16 inches

WINDOW PANE STRUTS

1 piece at
⅛ inch x ¼ inch x 20 inches

2 pieces at
¼ inch x ¼ inch x 12 inches

1 piece at
¼ inch x ¼ inch x 20 inches

ROOF TURRETS

shells

nut

tape

roof

bolt

CROSS SECTION

corner post

nails

floorboards

playhouse wall

ground

floor joists

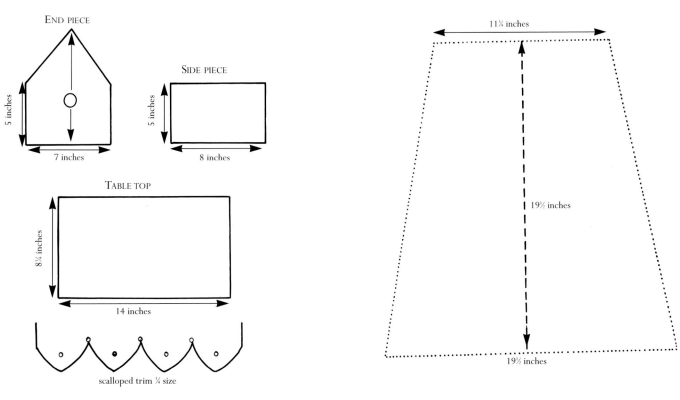

END PIECE

5 inches

7 inches

SIDE PIECE

5 inches

8 inches

TABLE TOP

8¼ inches

14 inches

scalloped trim ¼ size

BEACH-HUT BIRDHOUSE PP. 38-41

11¼ inches

19½ inches

19½ inches

LIMPET LAMP PP. 63-65

USEFUL ADDRESSES

ORGANIZATIONS

Boston Malacological Club
c/o The Shell Gallery
77 Union Street
Newton Center, MA 02159

Central Florida Shell Club
P.O. Box 10146
Pompano Beach, FL 33061

Conchological Club of
Southern California
c/o 900 Exposition Blvd.
Los Angeles, CA 90007

Jacksonville Shell Club
c/o 709 Lomax St.
Jacksonville, FL 32204

Long Island Shell Club
c/o Edna Lane
Dix Hills, NY 11746

National Audubon Society
900 Broadway
New York, NY 10003

San Diego Shell Club
c/o 3883 Mt. Blackburn Ave.
San Diego, CA 92111

AUTHOR'S ACKNOWLEDGMENTS

Thank you to Claire Andrews *(Beach-hut Birdhouse),* Andrew Gillmore *(Rock-pool Fountain, Scallop Plant Tidy, Playhouse by the Sea* and *Shelly Salad Servers)* and Bridget Morrall *(Limpet Lamp)* for making such great projects, and to Peter Williams for photographing them so beautifully. A special thank you to Andrew Gillmore for all his help and support, and to Mrs. F. Gillmore for collecting shells for me.

PUBLISHERS' ACKNOWLEDGMENTS

The publishers would like to thank Minicraft, Macford Products Ltd., 1-2 Enterprise City, Meadowfield Avenue, Spennymoor, Co Durham DH16 6JF, Tel: (01388) 420435, for lending us drills and attachments.

INDEX